Midnight of the Sublime

Midnight of the Sublime

·

ESSAYS & REVIEWS
BY
ALAN WALL

Odd Volumes

of the

The Fortnightly Review

Les Brouzils

2021

Copyright © Alan Wall. All rights reserved.

Odd Volumes of

The Fortnightly Review

www.fortnightlyreview.co.uk

Editorial office:
Château Ligny
2 rue Georges Clemenceau
85260 Les Brouzils
France

ODD VOLUMES 2021

ISBN 978-0-9991365-7-7

CONTENTS

1. The Poet as Essayist 1

2. No Worst There Is None 5

3. Note on Inscape, Descriptionism and Logical Form 15

4. Viduities 25

5. Shakespeare's Dysnarrativia 41

6. Considering 'I', Alone 57

7. Looking Back in Anger 67

8. Modernist Poetics 79

9. Ludwig Wittgenstein 105

10. Irony and Ironists 133

11. Hell 161

12. The Poet and the Dictionary 183

13. Textuality: Ephesus and Patmos 207

14. Tolerance and Form 239

PUBLISHER'S NOTE

This is the third volume of essays by Alan Wall published by Odd Volumes, the imprint of *The Fortnightly Review*. As with the first two collections, these are not academic essays. They are, however, scholarly and charged with the author's singular intelligence and literary skills.

They are what the author calls 'exercises in radical pattern-recognition'. Wall believes that the essay is the perfect form for provisional explorations and intellectual forays into the often bewildering realities of the world today. In his hands, the essay form is flexible and capacious, allowing for an engaging intellectual experimentalism which exhilarates and always avoids sliding into academic jargon and obfuscation. Most of Wall's essays are almost entirely unencumbered by footnotes. They are speedy, risk-taking pieces of writing. Each one is an urgent search for illumination. We are happy to provide this trilogy of thought-provoking essays to readers of *The Fortnightly Review*.

1.

The Poet as Essayist

I DISTRUST PEOPLE who write or talk as though they don't have bodies or histories, though it can result in a certain stateliness of tone. That is the realm of the grandiloquent, where it is all too easy to be suckered. If a fellow wants to divorce himself from his first-person singular, our wish to question that intimate pronoun might grow apace. Who is the *I* crouching behind the *We?* Why talk to us on stilts, guv'nor? Why do you want us always to look up, and never down? Stop booming; a whisper might be more believable. Some philosophers acknowledge their daily existence in the midst of their prose; others do not. I need to visit the kitchen, therefore I am.

It can depend on the matter at hand.

Euclid announces in Proposition 47 of Book I that the square on the hypotenuse is equal to the sum of the squares on the two opposing sides. Now I don't need to count the fellow's griefs or know which side he butters his toast on. This is definitive stuff. So in a different way is this:

> Of Man's first disobedience, and the fruit
> Of that forbidden tree whose mortal taste
> Brought death into the World, and all our woe,
> With loss of Eden, till one greater Man
> Restore us, and regain the blissful seat,
> Sing, Heavenly Muse…

I don't care how blind he is, or how he's been getting on lately with Mrs Milton. The story is bigger than the voice employed. If the theme is big enough, the first-person singular is swallowed by a larger force. Euclid's propositions balance up the world. As long as we limit its dimensions. Milton's imagined world traces the ætiology of our trauma. And we've already encountered most of the characters before, though some new ones introduce themselves in their allegorical uniforms. In both cases the form is equal to the pressure of the saying.

Look hard enough and you will see the form in the fragment.

Form is never incidental.

Form should always be central to our considerations. Some refer to Montaigne as a philosopher, but they are careless in doing so. Montaigne never wrote a work of systematic philosophy and seems to have been unwilling to do so. He was a thinker whose form was the essay. If we have to designate the overall pattern of his thought, it was essayism. Essayism cherishes the fragment, rather than disparaging it. Look hard enough and you will see the form in the fragment. Form is never incidental. Wittgenstein's prose does not join up. Each section keeps its distance from the others. These truths are wary of intermarriage. They are sceptical of holistic reconciliation. They say the truth itself appears in fragments.

Form is important because it shapes the thought it contains. Claude Lanzmann disparaged Steven Spielberg's *Schindler's List*. The problem with the film was its form. Can a Hollywood movie contain the truth of the Holocaust? No. It shapes the experience to facilitate its own function: to entertain, through characterisation and suspense for a limited time (three hours and fifteen minutes). Lanzmann's own filmic representation, *Shoah*, lasted nine and a half hours. There was no dramatic action in it. It was held together by the thematics of the Holocaust, historic testimonies, and the inquisitorial unrelentingness of the director. Hollywood movies also press towards comedic form: we long to see the couple leaving hand-in-hand at the finale. And so the Holocaust has a microcosmic happy ending. The macrocosmic reality (historically speaking) was a catastrophe. But the microcosm (this movie) finds a form of redemption. The generic nature of the form shapes the historical experience it is pursuing. And inevitably distorts it.

If you mistake the form then you mistake everything. Most conspiracy theories have a glimmer of truth in them. This is the barbed hook that the fish's mouth is snagged on. This is the bit where we can engage with the world as we know it; then we are led away into the grand conspiratorial halls, which Milton baptised pandemonium. As faith in conventional politics dwindles to a trickle, big theories showing who's really in charge take command. The wave increases as the official trickle diminishes to vanishing point. The form is dialectical; as one aspect swells the other contracts. Form here must be read in relation to the official propaganda it is supplanting. It is a function of larger ideological manoeuvres.

FORM CAN TEND to be nostalgic. The first train carriages imitated horse carriages. The first films tended to lean towards the theatrical. Charlie Chaplin stood midway between vaudeville and the cinematic screen. The true essayist insists that you cannot merely enlarge an essay to make a book. That is to travesty its form. Nor can you take a theatrical play and automatically turn it into a film. The form must be entirely re-thought. Neither *Waiting for Godot* nor *Rosenkrantz and Guildenstern Are Dead* make good films: the theatrical form remains too resounding inside the celluloid. If you make a film of 'The Ancient Mariner', you will produce a mere narrative; the poem is much more than a narrative, though narration remains at its core.

When George Oppen wrote *Of Being Numerous* in the 1960s, he was a writing a consciously, formally democratic verse. It fragments and recombines. It celebrates the 'shipwreck of the singular'. The *I* has been fractured. It is no more an isolated entity, a singularity that commands its world. The form of that marvellous poem utters its meaning. The short jagged lines shape themselves into crowds. These crowds are never queuing to see a throne. The 1960s spent a lot of time examining the *I*, for – as George Harrison would point out – life goes on within you and without you. As a poet, Oppen is an essayist. The essayist knows he can never portray the whole; it must always remain partial. We only ever get to see in glimpses and glimmers.

2.

No Worst There Is None

THE PATH TO Rome sounds like a splendid journey. You might start from some dilapidated suburb, drenched by Albion's parochial showers, but you end up entering the vivid sunshine of St Peter's Square. So much radiant symmetry. Then you can step inside and look up at Michaelangelo's vision of the beginning and end of things. Or look back down again and stare at his Pietà, in which the mother of Jesus would appear to be considerably younger than the redeemer himself. It's like one of those American cartoons where everything ends up exactly as it started, or slightly better, despite the myriad manglings that have gone on in between. This is the future perfect. This really is something to look forward to.

It wasn't always like that at all. What Gerard Manley Hopkins and others had to endure was more often a journey from a suburban and dull (but well-funded) church life to a sacramental booth for the proletariat, often immigrant, frequently sordid and unsavoury. Ugly churches filled with kitsch and tat, rudimentary accommodation in the presbytery, ancient leather furniture which had long before rotted and now sported leprous skin. A canon whose closest companion was whisky. The company could be seriously uncongenial. And the weekly rituals of confession did not bring the prodigal son back home, but merely enacted a rehearsal of the tawdry spiritual misdemeanours of the poor. And how those sins recurred – again and again and again.

After the leafy turreted city of Oxford, where his conversion took place, under the distant shadow of John Henry Newman, Gerard Manley Hopkins endured his priestly service in Sheffield, Manchester, Liverpool and Glasgow. As his correspondence makes clear, these could be grim enough places in the later nineteenth century. The poor teemed, procreated and suffered; they lean towards a notable consistency in this regard. And they went to see Father when their souls needed absolution; to wash away those gruesome offences that stained the inner life. A poem like 'Felix Randal' shows that Hopkins did not condescend to his parishioners. Like Jesus himself, he never played the superior to those who came to him, genuinely beseeching restoration and forgiveness.

Hopkins was a linguistic archaeologist, digging away at the present surface of the language to find the roots and remnants of energy beneath.

HE HAD CONVERTED to the Roman faith because he believed it brought him closer to the true source of his belief. It was a terrible wrench, effecting a breach with his family that never healed. But the wish to scrape away the patina of Anglican belief and find the original dogma underlying it was too strong. This passion never left him, despite the undoubted misery of his later years. And the wish to return to fundamentals was a prime impulse in his poetry too. For Hopkins was a linguistic archaeologist, digging away at the present surface of the language to find the roots and remnants of energy beneath. The real energy instinct in Victorian English, he believed, was Anglo-Saxon, and his verse sought, as far as possible, to reclaim that pre-Conquest vitality. To return to it on the page before him.

Hopkins understood well enough how splendid is the language of Shakespeare, or Chaucer before him. But he came to believe that the Old English heritage had been too great a loss, when the Normans arrived, bringing their linguistic gifts along with them. We see the merger at its most lucid in Chaucer. Here we note how the Romance morphologies have been grafted on to the native tongue, providing lexical ambivalence and flexibility. But there was a price (as there always is). Latinate diction takes one a step away from the reality denoted. It is a little less directly perceptual; a little more analytic. A preface is slightly daintier than a foreword, a sheep more rooted in its field than the mutton we slice out of it. There is something more urbane about improvement, compared to the betterment it once displaced. The ancestor has always made it further up the ladder than the forebear he elbowed out of the pecking order. The deer has to go to school before it can re-emerge, properly dressed at last, as venison. And although the displacement is now more or less complete, if you contradict me you are not as close to the native earth as if you gainsay me.

The above examples show the Anglo-Saxon usages have been in decline for centuries. The Romance words always sounded a little more professional, even a little more fragrant. The poor benighted pig on its final journey might well opt for the abattoir rather than the slaughterhouse. My own grandfather started off as a dustbinman, but later in life he was designated a refuse collector. Like Bottom, he had been translated. At its most egregious this practice can be seen when governments speak, at the precise time they would prefer to keep silent. So an American administration came up with 'collateral damage'. Translated, this means lots of people blown to bits that we weren't even aiming at. Think what a different world it would be if instead of psychology we turned to soul learning to help us through the remains of the day. 'It makes me weep to think what English might have been,' Hopkins wrote to Robert Bridges.

Hopkins never studied Old English as part of any course. He seems to have done it off his own bat. He was at Oxford when the study was blossoming, but he wrote to Bridges in 1882 (long after he had left Oxford), 'learning Anglosaxon and it is a vastly superior thing to what we have now.' The Early English Text Society was formed in 1864, and new versions of *Beowulf* were being produced. In 1851, R. C. Trench published his *Study of Words*, in which he argued that there had been a loss with the linguistic importations of the Norman invasion. Hopkins cobbled together all that he wanted from the Old English tradition. One thing he noticed, with luminous attention, was our early tradition of accentual metres.

HOPKINS HAS BECOME famous for a particular form of prosody: sprung rhythm. What this means at its simplest is verse that does not count its syllables, but its stresses. The Old English tradition had lines consisting of four strong stresses, separated in the middle by a caesura. The number of syllables involved was variable. Although not strictly syllabic, much English poetry is regular enough to be dominated by a strict count of poetic feet:

> The curfew tolls the knell of parting day,
> The lowing herd winds slowly o'er the lea…

Here five iambic pentameters structure each line. You could change some of the feet with substitutions and still retain the overall metre. But there are no extra syllables here so we have two ten-syllable lines. Hopkins found such a poetic convention constraining, not because of the wildness of his temperament, or his stormy emotions, but because the native vigour of the English language was being constrained by an imported tradition.

And in absorbing the Anglo-Saxon tradition, he took on board other aspects of it too. The compounding of words is a Germanic trait. Hopkins followed it. Compound words permit descriptive morphologies. A simple example. One word for body in Old English is *banhus*. Bonehouse. If you call your body a bonehouse, it has implications. What is being housed? Hopkins took what he wanted: he was never slavish. He said, in a letter, that faced with greatness his inclination was to admire and do otherwise. In another letter, he said the trick was to be independent but not unimpressionable. He formed his own compounds, as Paul Celan would later do in German with coinages like *Niemandsrose* and *Atemwende*. And along with the compounds, there was alliteration and assonance — a lot of both.

By 1884 Hopkins was in Dublin, a Professor of Greek and Latin, and thoroughly miserable. He would have preferred to be back in England, where he at least had some friends. He was hard-worked, and his natural conscientiousness would not let him ease up on the unceasing activities of preparing, lecturing, marking, and then starting the cycle all over again. His professorship sometimes felt to him like a dicky-bow on a corpse. Georgian Dublin was largely wrecked by the depredations of civic development. In the city of Guinness, he took no solace in drink. The five years left to him, before his early death in 1889, were never happy ones. Constantly suffering from ill health, with his eyesight fading, he battled on through his duties. And he wrote some of the darkest verse written in English. These are the poems that are sometimes called the terrible sonnets, and this is one of them:

> No worst, there is none. Pitched past pitch of grief,
> More pangs will, schooled at forepangs, wilder wring.
> Comforter, where, where is your comforting?
> Mary, mother of us, where is your relief?
> My cries heave, herds-long; huddle in a main, a chief-
> Woe, world-sorrow; on an age-old anvil wince and sing –
> Then lull, then leave off. Fury had shrieked 'No ling-
> Ering! Let me be fell: force I must be brief'.
>
>   O the mind, mind has mountains; cliffs of fall
> Frightful, sheer, no-man-fathomed. Hold them cheap
> May who ne'er hung there. Nor does long our small
> Durance deal with that steep or deep. Here! Creep,
> Wretch, under a comfort serves in a whirlwind: all
> Life death does end and each day dies with sleep.

> **One thing is immediately apparent: there is no point counting syllables here. The whole poem structures itself around stresses.**

One thing is immediately apparent: there is no point counting syllables here. The whole poem structures itself around stresses. The syllables hang around each stress, like iron filings patterned by a magnetic charge. The poem rushes its first line with the energy Donne employed in his *Songs and Sonnets*. We might also register a higher proportion of teutonic words than usual. Hopkins fought hard to keep the Latinate words out. Hence the phrase (which he struggled over in manuscript) 'no-man-fathomed'. He did not want *plumbed* and he did not want *explored*, both of which go back ultimately to Rome. So he fashioned his own phrase, entirely out of Old English words. The rhythm is sprung, no line is a dutiful syllable-counter, until the very end when the last three feet are regular iambs: 'and each day dies with sleep.' So, after all the turmoil that has preceded it, the sprung rhythm dies at last into the running rhythm. Regularity is restored — with death. Life demands more irregularity.

The savage economy of the phrasing relies on rhythmic pulse and elision. 'Hold them cheap/May who ne'er hung there.' If one gets rid of the elision, there is a somewhat more cumbersome statement: 'Those who have never been to these treacherous regions may disparage the horrors they hold.' One can see how paraphrase destroys the poetry. Mandelstam put it well: 'For where there is amenability to paraphrase, there the sheets have never been rumpled, there poetry has never spent the night.' Hopkins' economy of expression is possible because of his intensive reading, but also because of his intensive hearing. In 'Felix Randal', Hopkins writes: 'Ah well, God rest him all road ever he offended.' He heard that, in the phraseology of working men. The usage still survives in the northern phrase 'Any road up'. Hopkins is exercising extreme intelligence inside this text; he is helping the words to locate themselves with maximum vigour and force. This is the ultimate vindication of the task of the philologist-poet. To find eloquence not in smoothness, but in the jagged soundings of potent speech.

And it is potency that accounts for the repetitions. 'O the mind, mind has mountains...' This is the staccato vividness of thought, pursuing its own unending circularities. The mind drops its article in the next phrase 'mind has mountains'. They are 'frightful, sheer, no-man-fathomed' — all words pulled from the Anglo-Saxon lexicon. They might, at first glance, feel similar to 'caverns measureless to man', yet Coleridge's poem feels tranquil compared to Hopkins'. Here we have mental torment tracing its own feverish movements. Tracing them but incapable of escaping them.

Hopkins was a syntactical inventor. See how he conveys the hideous circularity of mental torment in another of the sonnets:

> My own heart let me more have pity on; let
> Me live to my sad self hereafter kind,
> Charitable; not live this tormented mind
> With this tormented mind tormenting yet.

This is a syntactical ouroboros, manically chewing its own tail. It snakes round and round. If we follow the circle's logic, there is no end in sight, only more and more beginnings.

> **Hopkins came to understand that, in poetry, there isn't a 'meaning', which language can merely allude to or employ; meaning must be embodied in language itself...**

Hopkins came to understand that, in poetry, there isn't a 'meaning', which language can merely allude to or employ; meaning must be embodied in language itself, dynamically rooted there. Language can too easily refer to a shadow, the shadow of something we call meaning. For this to be avoided, each copula must become incarnational. Hopkins saw clearly that the parables of Jesus are not true because of their content (which was folkloric) but their form. The content is a fabular base. It is the form which reverses the epistemology, and thereby alters the relations of reality. In the formal shift of expectations, there we find the truth. Representation without full linguistic engagement is little more than skidding on language, a trick involving rhythmic phraseology.

Hopkins insisted that his verse was for the ear not the eye. So he must have constantly recited it to himself. How else would one get to hear it? He probably walked the streets of Dublin uttering the verses to himself, until they came right. A few decades later, in St. Petersburg, Osip Mandelstam would walk up and down Gorki Street calling out his verse. As he himself observed, no one ever listened, even when he was reciting the 'Stalin Ode', the poem that led to his imprisonment, and ultimately his death. People, as ever, had other things to do.

Since we now live in a virtual age, perhaps we should devise a virtual memorial. One for Mandelstam on Gorki Street, making his improvised broadcasts, since he had been officially unpublishable since 1928. And one for Gerard Manley Hopkins on St Stephen's Green, reciting the terrible sonnets. A Roman Catholic priest in a Roman Catholic town calling out in anguish to a Roman Catholic God. The only comfort that came was in the shape of the poems beseeching it. No replies ever arrived. They were, as he so wonderfully put it, 'like dead letters sent to dearest him that lives alas! away'.

3.

A Note on Inscape, Descriptionism and Logical Form

TOWARDS THE END of the eighteenth century, Coleridge believed that there could be no conflict between rational endeavour and the tenets of a valid religion. His Unitarianism dispensed with the accoutrements of traditional Trinitarian Christianity. His radical politics dispensed with the absurdities of antique social pomp and structure. And his poetry, along with that of Wordsworth, sought a language unfettered by the triteness and pat phrasing of clichéd allusiveness and poeticism. It seemed for a moment that all forms of genuine intellectual endeavour were pointing in the same direction. As Coleridge remarked in his notebooks, if new knowledge conflicts with established belief, then established belief had better shift itself to accommodate the recent intellectual discoveries.

In 1879, Gerard Manley Hopkins first used the word 'inscape' to describe how forms in nature or art express themselves through the luminosity and precision of their language.

A hundred years later the situation was radically different. And yet there was still a clamour to achieve clarity of language and formal precision of thought, in both art and science. It was in 1879 that Gerard Manley Hopkins first uses the word 'inscape' in a letter, to describe how forms in nature or art express themselves through the luminosity and precision of their language. Three years later, in 1882, Ernst Mach first employed the idea of science being 'economy of thought', and at the same time Frege was developing the notion of 'logical form', a sense of the sharing of formal identity between sundry modes of expression by means of formal homology. Karl Pearson's *The Grammar of Science* first appeared in 1892, but the thoughts it contained had been circulating over the previous two decades. This was a way of thinking known as Descriptionism, which believed that science explained nothing, and should not attempt to. All it could do was describe, with scrupulous exactitude and logically scrubbed language. Even words like *cause* and *causality* arrive carrying metaphysical implications. Many of these debates were carried on in the pages of the *Fortnightly Review*.

It was Wittgenstein who took up where G.W. Frege had left off in regard to logical form. What do a performed piece of music, the score for that music, and a vinyl record of the same all have in common? Logical form. The way the notes are arranged on the page, the height and depth of the grooves on the record, and the combined effect of all the instruments generating sound waves during a performance, all share something: the logical form that expresses a central identity, namely the structure of the composition itself. We might also note that in 1879, the same year Hopkins wrote his letter to Bridges employing the word *inscape*, Cézanne was painting *The Bridge at Maincy*, in which he finds in nature the geometry underlying it, and he struggles to portray it in paint. This is economy of thought, expressed in art not science. Nor does it seek to explain, in any allegorical manner: this is descriptionism rendered in pigment. This is how form encounters subject in a specific modality.

As any scientist knows, economy of thought is useless without economy of notation. And notation, through its silent endeavours, can generate thought. To write is not merely to memorialize a pre-existing thought: writing is a cognitive activity, and generates its own intellectual heuristics. To formulate the perfect proposition is to find a correlate between the natural world as we are able to perceive and understand it, and a way of expressing those relations in linguistic or mathematical form. This applies to Wittgenstein's early propositions. It also applies to Hopkins' notion of inscape: a logic of coherent expression, a structured principle of articulated lucidity. The exploration of the appropriate form is the expression of inscape in a particular medium. It is a discovery in the shape of expression that bespeaks an inscape. Inscape in art elicits a perceptible and coherent identity in the perceived object or situation. And, in propositional terms, if this set of words describes this situation adequately, logical form is shared between words and situation. To formulate a valid proposition means to make language conform to the facts of the situation. All the facts of all the situations are what Wittgenstein called 'the world'.

In the *Tractatus*, Wittgenstein writes: 'Form is the possibility of structure.' Form announces what the structural possibilities are, though the process can often be dialectical. For example, the word atom announces that the entity designated has no structure. It is *atomos*, and therefore indivisible. In 1897, Thompson discovered the electron. That meant the atom did have a structure after all. And in 1911 Rutherford encountered the nucleus. Although we have stuck with the word atom, its etymology now contradicts what we know about its structure, and therefore its form. The concept of the form has had to be adjusted in relation to discoveries about the structure. Neither Thompson nor Rutherford were looking for what they found. Their knowledge was securely harboured until it broke its moorings. Then they had to rethink the 'form of the atom'. Our forms of knowing often need fracturing. We settle into them like lime casings. Wallace Stevens put it well:

> It is as if
> We had come to the end of the imagination,
> Inanimate in an inert savoir.

'An inert savoir' is a wonderful phrase for knowingness. Knowingness is lethal for any serious endeavour in science or art. If you already know, what on earth would be the point of searching? Any genius is a genius at not knowing. Isaac Newton was the only fellow in Lincolnshire during a plague year who did not know why an apple fell to the ground when it snapped off the twig. Everyone else knew. 'That's what apples do, Izzie. Apples go down; birds go up. Don't have to go to Cambridge to crack that one, sunshine. Might as well stay here in your stepfather's orchard. Picking apples.' But Isaac stuck with his not-knowing, even though it made him gauche. The others went on as usual, 'inanimate in an inert savoir.' He wrote *Philosophiæ Naturalis Principia Mathematica*.

The diagrammatic quality of Cubism makes the images it created the most supremely intellectual endeavours in the history of art.

WE CANNOT THINK about atoms without using diagrams. Photographs are problematical; no lens is fast enough to record sub-atomic movements, and our photographic intrusion alters what we are perceiving. At the same moment that Rutherford was confronted with the nucleus in 1911, art was moving in a diagrammatic direction. This movement was called Cubism. A diagram is not committed to a particular moment in time, in the way an illusionistic painting is. It can examine functions from different viewpoints and combine them. The first time people saw Cubist pictures in Paris, the nearest model to what they had been looking at could well have been the diagrams of Leonardo da Vinci. Here, in assembled and exploded form, a machine would be taken apart, and then put back together. All in a single image. The Cubists disassembled the unitary composite held in the sensorium, and displayed the individual components. They were trying to get rid of the spurious causality of the illusionistic image. They were being as mechanical as possible with the elements of vision. Like the Descriptionists, they wanted to hunt down the various glues and adhesives with which we hold our visions together, and put them under severe questioning. The diagrammatic quality of Cubism makes the images it created the most supremely intellectual endeavours in the history of art. And the process of visual analysis began, as both Picasso and Braque fully acknowledged, with Cézanne.

So we have Cézanne in painting; Hopkins in poetry; Frege in logic, and Wittgenstein in philosophy, all within decades of each other striving to achieve the same thing in different fields: a lucidity and economy of thought and description which cuts away all inessentials, so as to present us with luminous facts, luminous because their light is unimpeded by clutter. Brancusi spoke of the break from realism to modernism as a release from that 'confusion of familiarities'. Pearson in *The Grammar of Science* spoke of 'the routine of our perceptions'. If we furnish our minds with a clutter of familiarities then we will, to use Blake's phrase, only see with the eye, not through it. Wittgenstein was better suited to navigate his way through this world than his fellow students at Cambridge, because his education had been diagrammatic.

The undergraduates around him at Cambridge had been trained in the classics. Wittgenstein had been trained in engineering, studying how machines work, seeing how to fix them, devising ways to make them function better. The way of thinking through these problems was the diagram. Probably providing him with his first realisation that what you can show with great clarity you can't necessarily say at all. At the Technische Hochschule in Charlottenberg, Wittgenstein learned to think diagrammatically. Theorizing was a last resort; first, you had to grasp the practice. We see the result in the *Tractatus*: propositions are assembled and exploded, as in a competent diagram. He thought as an engineer about the engineering of language. He was searching for the recurrent inscape of meaning. His mind attuned itself to the occupation of logical space.

There is another way of putting this. All the main characters in the constellation sketched above, in their radically different fields, were hunting for significant form. Significant form is an escape from that choral confusion of familiarities that can come to constitute daily life, and its routine of perception. Routines of perception so easily become 'an inert savoir'.

The phrase was first used by Clive Bell in 1914. It was part of the endeavour he shared with Roger Fry, to grasp the potency of post-impressionist painting. Both saw Cézanne as the key figure. He had foregrounded formal arrangement, so that in his paintings the formalities of composition transcend the significance of subject-matter. A pot, a glass, a flower, a table, become epic in their proportions, because they provide all that is necessary for the formal imagination, the ultimate wit of the artistic decoder, to discover and enact significant form. As Flaubert put it: '…everything in art depends on the execution: the story of a louse can be as fine as the history of Alexander the Great.' There is no hierarchy of subjects. Method and form reign supreme.

For Hopkins, inscape exists in nature, and it can also be achieved in language; it is as though the old Doctrine of Signatures had never died. The connection between the two, though he did not employ this language, is logical form. Homologous structures, in whatever medium, share it. And how can it be expressed? Through a precision of language, dispensing with all cluttering confusions of familiarity. Does a match cause a flame? No. A certain configuration of chemicals, excited by friction, will ignite. If there is any causality here, it is probably human.

> **Inscape defamiliarizes, by ridding the mind of intellectual bric-à-brac. This is why Picasso said that in modern art there was no past or future...**

Inscape defamiliarizes, by ridding the mind of intellectual bric-à-brac. This is why Picasso said that in modern art there was no past or future, and that such art was tied to no particular place or time. Form rules, and it abolishes time with a brushstroke. A man ravaged by desire becomes a minotaur, even if buses pass on the street outside. Form transcends temporal and spatial conventions. A radical grasp of form, an ability to articulate it within a given medium, achieves what the Russian Formalists were later to call defamiliarization. The confusion of familiarities is banished. Though we must always be wary. We say defamiliarization, but that is not exactly what Shklovsky wrote. He wrote *ostranenie*, which would be more accurately translated as making strange.

THE STATEMENTS THAT make up Wittgenstein's *Tractatus* exhibit a propositional clarity. They are not joined together by connective discourse. And there is a parallel between this ascetic search for logical form in a philosophical treatise, and what happens in Ezra Pound's poem 'In a Station of the Metro'. What had been thirty lines of discursive verse whittled itself down to a two-line poem of propositional clarity:

> The apparition of these faces in the crowd;
> Petals on a wet, black bough.

The perception starts out being analogous, and yet its final form makes it seem homologous, so appropriate does the relationship between the two images finally appear. They have achieved a significant form that grafts them on to one another, as though they were organically related, or at least symbiotically fused. The space between them ceases to be homogeneous, and becomes shaped instead. Homology signifies a shared origin in function and development. For example, pectoral fins, bird wings, and the forelimbs of mammals – all are homologous, whereas bird wings and insect wings are merely analogous. They share a function, not an origin.

The assumption that law lies behind all phenomena could be seen as theological, but it is also the assumption that drove physics during these years.

In his journal, Hopkins wrote: 'The shores are swimming and the eyes have before them a region of milky surf but it is hard for them to unpack the huddling and gnarls of the water and law out the shapes and sequence.' His confidence that the shapes and sequence could be 'lawed out' is as scientific as it is poetic, even though here it is contradicting the Second Law of Thermodynamics. The assumption that law lies behind all phenomena could be seen as theological, but it is also the assumption that drove physics during these years. Pattern-recognition is a training that leads to the detection of inscape; it also constitutes the scientific accumulation of knowledge that results in the annunciation of a law. The laws thus sought are the laws of nature. The inscape of those laws would finally express itself in the Solvay conference in 1927, with the formulation of quantum theory. Einstein thought there was altogether too much contingency here, and not enough causality. He never bought it. Not enough had been 'lawed out', as far as he was concerned.

One tends not to speak of the linguistic turn in relation to poetry; instead we speak of modernism. The linguistic turn was a foregrounding of language in all cognitive activities. Pound's two lines show how a vivid image, expressed in vivid language, can escape the cluttering discourse that usually surrounds it, which can also be expressed as Pearson's routine of our perceptions. Hopkins criticised a painting by Holman Hunt, saying that he could find no inscape in it. There was an excess of realistic detail, but no significant form either perceived or constructed. Inscape for Hopkins is the signature of order imprinted into every item of creation. To perceive it, we need to see through the eye not with it. It used to be perceived, if a little fancifully, through the Doctrine of Signatures.

In the visual arts this momentum into a complex clarity would arrive at Cubism. Cubism sought an exit from illusionism. Art should not be a machinery to pretend two dimensions are really three (or even four). Instead it should instruct the eye how it connives in half-constructing our vision. How the image is not merely given; it is also manufactured in the sensorium.

Wordsworth put it well:

...of all the mighty world
Of eye, and ear, – both what they half create,
And what perceive.

4.

Viduities

IN *KRAPP'S LAST TAPE*, Beckett presents us with Krapp listening to the tape-recordings of his own voice from many years before. Suddenly, he stops the spool and plays it back. The word that has snagged in his mind is *viduity*. He used it once, and so must once have known its meaning, but he does not appear to know its meaning any more. He goes backstage into darkness and returns with 'an enormous dictionary', in which he discovers – or rediscovers – that the word signifies 'State – or condition – of being – or remaining – a widow – or widower.' Krapp finds himself a little baffled by that phrase 'being or remaining', and repeats it.

He is right of course: the word *be* here contains the word *remains* (though the wording remains identical in the OED to this day). The life of Helen Thomas might have clarified his thoughts on the matter, since she became (and remained) one of the exemplary widows of the twentieth century. She played the faithful Penelope to the memory of one who did not return, as Odysseus did, from the great battle of his time, but died instead in the Great War of 1914-1918. This was the poet Edward Thomas, who only truly became a poet during the war years, and yet was not what we normally call a war poet.

Within six years of America's twentieth-century involvement, there were said to be three million spiritualists in America…

There had never been such a sprouting of spiritualism since its birthing years of 1848 to 1854 in the U.S., when the Fox family of Hydesville got things moving swiftly upwards through the astral planes, with the knocking sounds of spirits from the other side. Within six years of America's twentieth-century involvement, there were said to be three million spiritualists in America, their communicative urges dutifully serviced by ten thousand mediums. Now once again, as the Great War ground on, there had been séances held every night in one great city or another. The number of those who suddenly discovered a gift for establishing contact with the other side, or receiving messages therefrom, was effectively beyond counting. The Society for Psychical Research had been formed in 1882, by Frederic W. H. Myers and Edmund Gurney. And there were those, like W. B. Yeats, who believed it was only a matter of time before the existence of beings in a life beyond this one would be securely established. Scientific proof would be forthcoming; they were in no doubt of that.

Already there were photographs of the dead as they appeared during their sojourns amongst us. Particular photographic techniques, such as superimposition, played their part in this. And the sales of luminous cheesecloth rocketed, as ectoplasm in darkened rooms announced that, *pace* Hamlet, death was not that bourn from which no traveller returns.

Arthur Conan Doyle was at the centre of all this, fascinated by mesmerism, and the possibilities of different planes of existence, though one does not need Sherlockian gifts to diagnose the causes of such a huge expansion in the spiritualist trade in time of war, an expansion which was to carry on well into the 1930s. This was the most devastating war in history. So many who had been vividly alive a year or so before now lay dead. But it seemed that the conversation with them had to continue, so how precisely might that be achieved? It is a curiosity of the English language that if I am dealing with more than one organ of mass communication, then I must refer to media, but if I am addressing a gallimaufry of spiritualist communicators I must call them mediums. This usage is first recorded in the OED in 1851 in the U.S. The report concerned those 'rappings' that soon became such a salient feature of the séance. Those beings that had passed over were nothing if not percussive.[1]

Roman Jakobson listed the requirements for a successful communication thus:

- there must be an addresser and an addressee

- there must be a referent and a code through which it may be reached

- there must be the contact, or physical means by which the message itself is to be conveyed from addresser to addressee.

So what happens, we are entitled to ask, if the addressee is reported missing in action, but the urge to communicate with him remains as strong post-mortem as it had been before the presumed fatality? One possibility is that what Jakobson calls the contact has to be substantially modified so as to take the recent death into account. The physical addressee is replaced by an enhanced contact or physical channel; in other words, the medium expands to fill the space allotted to it, for in this instance, the medium is the message. The medium in the shape of a psychic facilitator has arrived. Through the preternaturally endowed communicator the barrier between the living and the dead may be broken down. Conan Doyle put it thus in one of his notebooks:

The end and aim of spiritual intercourse is to give man the strongest of all reasons to believe in spiritual immortality of the soul, to break down the barrier of death, to found the grand religion of the future.'

All you need is one who is enhanced by the requisite sensitivities to the relevant vibrations, the whisperings, the rappings. This was a time, we should recall, when it had dawned on humanity that our realm of perception was radically delimited. We might live inside the visible spectrum, within our own circumscribed audible limits, but there was plenty going on outside those parameters. Even a dog hears sounds too high-pitched ever to register in the human auditory system. Because you cannot see infrared or ultraviolet with the naked eye does not mean those regions of the spectrum do not exist. They are packed with information we can only access by special means. In other words, we need to discover the right medium of enquiry.

Jakobson also lists the six functions of communication, one of which is the conative. This is the mode of second-person address, the vocative I-Thou, which articulates communication in the intimate space of a direct address. This function occurs more frequently in verse and song than in prose (except in the epistolary form). And we note how frequently the addressee in the conative mode, particularly in verse, can be either dead or entirely deaf to our multiple entreaties. Jakobson nowhere addresses the significance of this, but it forms a substantial portion of our cultural inheritance. We have spent so much time talking either to the non-respondent gods, or to the dead, frequently in verse. What does this tell us about ourselves and our culture? Physical absence in perpetuity, it appears, in no way precludes our earnest communication.

DEAD LETTERS.

IN HIS POEM 'I wake and feel the fell of dark', Gerard Manley Hopkins writes:

> And my lament
> Is cries countless, cries like dead letters sent
> To dearest him that lives alas! away.

What does it mean to engage the conative function with an addressee who never answers: who seemingly cannot answer (in the human rubric) and yet must still be obsessively addressed? What does it mean to intone a psalm to Adonai, never expecting a reply? What does it mean to write poems addressing the Almighty (as

Hopkins did) to which no reciprocal communication will ever be despatched? The Dead Letter Office to which Hopkins alludes was a necropolis of failed communications. This was where mail that could not be delivered ended up, often waiting there for years before the enigma of the addressee could finally be resolved. So what exactly does it signify to be talking to the dead? Or, for that matter, to so ventriloquize the dead that they would appear once more to be talking to us? Practising as a doctor in Portsmouth, long before the Great War, Conan Doyle had held a séance in which a commercial traveller asked that his family in Slattenmere in Cumbria be connected on his behalf. Doyle duly wrote and posted the letter as requested. There was no such place as Slattenmere, and the letter came back finally, via the Dead Letter Office.

To every action there is an equal and opposite reaction: this is Newton's Third Law of Motion. But it would appear to apply far beyond the world of mechanics, or we might perhaps surmise that all realms have a secret system of mechanics governing them which, like the ultraviolet and the infrared, is all too frequently invisible to us. The expansion of postal services in the nineteenth century was phenomenal; it was their reliable multiple deliveries each day that facilitated the work of scientists like Charles Darwin. But such a massive expansion of postal communication produced an equal and opposite expansion of postal non-communication, and the emblematic black hole of this universe of missed connections was the Dead Letter Office.

The means of communication between soldiers in the trenches at the Western Front and their loved ones back in Blighty were letters and postcards. And then the dread communication might be delivered in the form of a telegram: Regret to inform you…. So this one too had gone.

A poem can be a kind of funerary monument, fashioned in words instead of stone.

Another husband, father, son or brother had stepped out of the air to join the fallen. When Helen Thomas received hers, it said that Edward had died on 9th April 1917. He had been killed by a shell-blast at the start of the Arras offensive. A month later Helen wrote to Robert Frost and his wife in America: '…how rich I am in his love & his spirit & all that is eternal, & all that was & is between us that he said again & again "Remember whatever happens all is well between us forever".' In other words, although he has died in body, he has not died in spirit, for the true spirit is eternal. Our funerary monuments tell us as much. And a poem can be a kind of funerary monument, fashioned in words instead of stone. The elegy is a continuance beyond death of the one who is seemingly lost forever. This is the burden of Milton's lines about Edward King in 'Lycidas':

Weep no more, woeful shepherds, weep no more
For Lycidas your sorrow is not dead…

The dead, when they are significant enough, enter the region of anamnesis. And significance here means love.

ANAMNESIS.

DAVID JONES SERVED in the Great War too, and he was also the recipient of the enemy's shrapnel. But he survived. He survived to spend the rest of his life pondering those great events, and what they signified about humanity, 'for Anthropos is not always kind'. He became a Roman Catholic, a poet, painter and essayist. And one of the terms he came to use more and more was anamnesis. The word means deliberated recollection; a calling-to-mind. It takes many cultural forms. One which was central to Jones was the anamnesis of the Catholic Mass. Do this in memory of me, said Jesus, in the cenacle on the first Maundy Thursday. Thus do I command you towards the accomplishment of this, my anamnesis.

One of Jones's great sources for his contemplation of anamnesis was Maurice de la Taille, and his book *Mysterium Fidei*. De la Taille argued that on the Thursday night in the upper room, Jesus had 'entered the order of signs'. What he then enacted in brute factuality the following day on the cross he had already enacted in the realm of sign on the night before. The implications of this for Jones's thought are incalculable. His work from then on was in effect based upon it. Humans are the sign-making creatures. We create tools but such objects are – in Jones's terminology – utile. When we create art we are fashioning the inutile; we are in effect engaging in an intransitive activity, an activity whose sole purpose is celebratory or reverential. This is the unique realm of sign-making. Like the Almighty, in art we engage in gratuitous creation. Another of Jones's sources, Jacques Maritain's *Art et Scolastique*, played down the distinction between art and artefacture. It was the identity of *homo faber* as maker that was significant, so that even our utile fashionings tend to spill over into the inutile. The sword might be meant to stab, but the decorations on its hilt or the damascene etchings on its blade serve no immediately lethal purpose. They are gratuitous too. Grace notes to the main theme of warfare.

All culture is based on memory. As Jones was fond of remarking, 'If you wish to insult the Muse, forget.'

All culture is based on memory. As Jones was fond of remarking, 'If you wish to insult the Muse, forget.' A chronicle is only meaningful if we can retain the sense of what went before, and the same applies to a novel. You cannot understand this page unless you retain remembrance of previous pages. Whatever we designate due matter for anamnesis is what we deem unforgettable. All cultures surround their most treasured anamneses with ritual. Ritual is a physical form of remembering. In the Christian cultus to which Jones subscribed, the Eucharistic sacrifice at the heart of the Mass is the central event of life, to be repeated daily. The voluntary self-immolation of Jeshua of Nazareth ordained the religion that was to follow in his name. And he had proclaimed that ordination the night before when he entered the order of signs by instituting the Eucharistic meal for his disciples.

All poetry is memorial. It calls to mind and litanizes that which must not be forgotten; that which the poet, as cultural remembrance, is exhorting us to recall. So we have Yeats in 1916:

> I write it out in a verse –
> Macdonagh and Macbride
> And Connolly and Pearse

> Now and in time to be
> Wherever green is worn,
> Are changed, changed utterly:
> A terrible beauty is born.

And here again is Edward Thomas:

> If I should ever by chance grow rich
> I'll buy Codham, Cockridden, and Childerditch,
> Roses, Pyrgo, and Lapwater,
> And let them all to my elder daughter.

They are both doing the same thing, and both doing it in the same year, 1916. Litanies present themselves as life-saving repetitions. They remind us, to use the words of David Jones once more, that we must work within the limits of our love. And the central act of anamnesis will be illocutionary: we utter the words that incant the desiderated action or presence. We build the temple out of stone in order that the spirit should inhabit it; we build the temple out of words (litany or poem) so as to welcome the spirit home. The beloved being is brought back into focus on the altar of our rite. This is re-calling, re-membering, re-collecting. I have made a heap of all that I could find, wrote Nennius, one of Jones's primary sources. These fragments I have shored against my ruins, wrote T. S. Eliot, with the ruined landscapes of the Great War forming a backdrop to his words.

CREATING A PSYCHIC SPACE.

IT TOOK TEN years for Robert Graves to publish his war memoir, *Goodbye to All That*, and the same amount of time for

Remarque's *All Quiet on the Western Front* to appear. David Jones had to find his own form, *In Parenthesis*, in which verse expands into prose, and prose contracts into verse on virtually every page. In *The Great War and Modern Memory*, Paul Fussell claims that the shock of the war was so great that a new form of remembering had to be invented in order to hold it in remembrance; a form had to be found in which to write it out. This is parallel to Freud's argument in *Beyond the Pleasure Principle* that the unexpectedness of the war meant that it was never prepared for in the psyche. That which has been prepared for need not leave a trace; but that which is both shocking and unexpected leaves a trace, an experiential cicatrix in the mind's flesh, because no mechanism of psychological acceptance had been prepared to receive the experience, with its traumatic potential. Freud came to believe that the endless reliving of war experience as trauma and dream was a way of retrospectively coping with the trauma. The calling to mind here was involuntary, so it was not anamnesis in Jones's sense. A man returned from the front, having suffered neurasthenia (or, as the soldiers called it, shell-shock), shouting out in the night or losing control of his functions, was not engaged in anamnesis. This deranged recurrence was involuntary; not a litany, then, but a pathology. The mind was in effect shouting out: I had never been prepared for this, and must now belatedly prepare the psychic ground. Some of the suffering had been so severe that no one could ever have been ready for it. Those like Jones who subsequently underwent forms of psychotherapy were attempting to return to the trenches through recollection, in order to re-encounter the horrors, this time with a precognition which history had at last vouchsafed.

THE TERRORS OF THE DEAD.

THE CENTRAL STATEMENT of the Mass is the priest's utterance: 'This is my body'. The tense is present. He does not, after all, say, 'This was my body', though Jesus has been certifiably crucified these last two thousand years. The words, taken from that ceremony where the order of signs was first entered, utter a presence. He who was dead is now living. The words of the liturgy are performative.

We are outnumbered by the dead. Should they all return at once, our world would be crowded, perhaps beyond endurance. Bob Hope waits in cryonic suspension, ready for that moment when the medical technology can restore him to the ranks of the living, where he might once more set the table on a roar, as Yorick too had done, before they laid him in the earth, before digging him up again. A prolepsis of archaeology. The earth holds the dead for us, like a safe deposit box, until we are ready to bring them out into the light once more, thus to begin our painstaking analysis.

The earth holds the dead for us, like a safe deposit box, until we are ready to bring them out into the light once more, thus to begin our painstaking analysis.

The idea of encountering the dead has haunted poetry from its beginnings. The first real poem we ever created was Gilgamesh. In that the mighty ruler has to confront the fact that his beloved companion, Enkidu, has died, and gone to the dreadful region where the dead are punished, not with judgment, but merely with the hideous reality of imprisonment in the land of the dead, where you are dressed as birds in black feathers, and must eat dirt. There is no escape from this fate; cryonics have not yet made their entry. In Book 11 of *The Odyssey*, Odysseus travels to the place where members of the Underworld might be met. The shades arrive, hungry for the blood he offers. It is evident that the greatest blessing they might receive is forgetfulness. Then there is Book 6 of *The Aeneid*, where Aeneas travels to the land of the dead. And then there is Dante's *Inferno*, where the dead really do get their just desserts.

SOLARIS.

ONE OF THE most extraordinary evocations of the dead, and the illocutionary force with which the psyche might summon them, is *Solaris*. This is the film made by Andrei Tarkovsky from the novel by Stanislaw Lem, who came to regard the film as a travesty of his book and very nearly disowned it. In both film and book a new planet has managed somehow to insert itself into the solar system. It constitutes a sea of liquid gas. In its vicinity curious occurrences take place. The most curious of them is that the dead come back to life, reconstituted apparently as a ghostly physiology of neutrinos. Even if you destroy the revenant once more, he or she will rapidly be reconstituted. They are infinitely reconstitutable, and amnesiac. Their only connection to memory is the remembrance of those to whom they are attached. They are like a prosthetic manifestation of the memory of the other.

> **The dead appear to be activated by the psychic potencies of those whose obsessions resurrect them. The return is not necessarily welcome.**

The dead appear to be activated by the psychic potencies of those whose obsessions resurrect them. The return is not necessarily welcome. Kelvin tries to fire his dead wife Hari back to earth on a rocket, so he might be rid of her in perpetuity. But she returns the next day. His own troubled remembrance, it seems, cannot be so easily shortcircuited by its own manoeuvres. She is the reincarnation of the troubled part of his memory in which she subsists. She has a home there which cannot be demolished. And one of the questions the film asks is this: how much do we really want the dead to return? If Bob Hope were to arise now from his sepulchre of chilled hydrogen, having been sustained in his state of cryopreservation, would we really thank him for the memory? Or, like Kelvin with Hari, would we try to find a means of disposing of him once more? What was it like at the evening meal that Martha and Mary prepared for their brother, Lazarus? What questions do you ask? 'So, what's it like being dead then?'

REMEMBERING THE REMEMBERED

'DO THIS IN memory of me.' Thus Jesus, on the first Sheer Thursday feast, inaugurating his own anamnesis. And Geoffrey Hill at the beginning of his magisterial poem 'The Mystery of the Charity of Charles Péguy' has these lines:

> ....Must men stand by what they write
> as by their camp-beds or their weaponry
> or shell-shocked comrades while they sag and cry?

The text of memory might demand more of us than we are ready to give. And when a writer dies, it is the texts that remain. Helen Thomas began to memorialize her husband, who had so effectively memorialized beloved parts of the English landscape, turning topography into a kind of liturgy. She did not pretend that the memorializing was unproblematical. Thomas was a difficult man, and knew it. With downswings of mood so dreadful that they placed a curse not only on him, but on all in his vicinity. His poems of 1916 can be seen as partly penitential: a making amends for his failures as husband and father.

But Helen loved him; loved him enough not to sentimentalize him. She tried to see him steadily and see him whole. She knew the poetry had come out of pain as much as exhilaration.

It is notable how religious the language of memorializing the fallen in times of war often is. The sacrificial self-immolation of Christ seems echoed in the sacrifice of the serving soldier. Blood spilt can still make the land sacred, though perhaps with less conviction as each fresh year goes by. Modern warfare still links up with primitive rituals. To repeat David Jones's remark, to insult or even widow the Muse, all you have to do is forget. Or designate memory a region for prosthetic devices, to be cached inside computers and in cyberspace clouds. The price of her viduity will be the shallowing-out of all our lives.

5.

Shakespeare's dysnarrativia

Dysnarrativia: the moment when language, or one language, breaks down, for internal or external reasons, leaving us unable to tell the established story of ourselves.

On 6 December 1273, Thomas Aquinas informed his faithful secretary, Brother Reginald, that he would write no more. This indefatigable author had turned over his last sheet. Reginald was taken aback. Why? Because, said Thomas, all he had written seemed to him nothing now but straw. He had received a vision of the divine plenitude, and there was a disjunction between the intensity of that vision and the resources available to human language.

His language could no longer tell the story of himself in any way that mattered, since it could not recount the single greatest event he had experienced. This condition is *dysnarrativia*.

Shakespeare is an expert portrayer of dysnarrativia. When language buckles inside the human mechanism, when discourse is traumatically disrupted so that the channels of disclosure and command are blocked, then we observe a linguistic metamorphosis. This can sometimes be redemptive, as with Lear and Leontes, but it is often dark and destructive. Sometimes grammar disintegrates. The lexicon turns vicious and anarchic.

LADY MACBETH.

IF WE CANNOT tell the story of ourselves, we cannot tell the story of others either. 'Tis all in pieces. All coherence gone', wrote John Donne in 1611, five years after Lady Macbeth's obsessive dreaming took place. The motors that are expected to push narrative along have broken down.

It is part of Shakespeare's genius that he grasps how, as the conscious mind loses its narrative coherence, the unconscious starts to take over.

Between her confident 'A little water clears us of this deed' and her later tragic utterance 'What is done cannot be undone' lies a break in narrative and narrativity so severe that it causes Lady Macbeth's death. It is part of Shakespeare's genius that he grasps how, as the conscious mind loses its narrative coherence, the unconscious starts to take over. In Lady Macbeth's sleepwalking dream the dreadful deeds are replayed in all their horror. The mind has not accepted her royal command of erasure and oblivion. She relives the horror that brought the prior narrative to such a brutal closure. She believed she could enforce closure upon history too, as Stalin believed he could erase Trotsky from all memories of the Russian Revolution. But history, interior and exterior, is not so easily erased. Like the watercourse dammed and diverted, it awaits the full flow of its future revenge. Those doctored photographs were one representation of history; but others were already in the post.

Freud came to believe that the recurrence of trauma in soldiers returning from the Great War was a form of belated rehearsal; the mind was trying to prepare itself *post factum* for that which it had not been prepared for when it actually occurred. The mechanized slaughter of the conflict surprised and astounded the western sensorium; it had no way of knowing this was coming. So it had to make amends for such lack of preparation in neurosis, nightmare and repetition. They had not volunteered for this, those poor benighted infantrymen. But Lady Macbeth had. She chose her actions with deliberation, even against her pliable husband's wishes. So the dysnarrativia that afflicted both the returning soldiers and her ladyship is different in kind. One was passive; the other active. Lady Macbeth willed what the Austrian soldiers merely had to endure. But she had no proleptic knowledge of the force her will was unleashing; she did not understand then, as she does later, that 'what is done cannot be undone'. What she appears to be rehearsing, in her later dreamwalking, is the unpreparedness of her will to perpetrate such an enormity, despite her vehement insistence at the time that it was ready for anything in order to fulfil ambition.

FREUD WAS OBSESSED by the childlessness of Lady Macbeth; he seemed to sense that here lies the clue to her character. It is as though a world that had voided itself of her (presumably male) child, the child that had once made the void of her womb swell, can now be voided of all order and sanctity in the form of the blessed Duncan, whom she helps murder. She can now assume the lethal manhood her own erased son had been denied; except of course that she doesn't. Those very sensations and thoughts she herself would denounce as womanish return upon her, first in conscious thought and then in the unwilled repetition of dream. The unconscious can still grasp a narrative that has fractured in the conscious realm. Thus did Shakespeare anticipate Freud by four centuries.

The unconscious is a space free of morality; its only dictates are impulse and desire, but even there, memory cannot be evacuated so easily. The unconscious memorializes as it desires; its objects are provided by the sensual world presented to the sensorium, ravished as they may be by wishes deemed illicit in the conscious world.

The death of the child has become a uterine negation. 'Bring forth man children only' says Macbeth. But she will bring forth nothing. She will beget nothing but death. The re-runs of the slaughter she choreographed now fill her midnight sensorium. The light that must be kept glowing at all times beside her bed cannot obliterate this darkness. The figures shrouded in darkness in this play never stop moving. They function like the *illuminati* of the darker powers.

Macbeth must assassinate the future: he remembers too much of it.
His imagination is paralysingly proleptic.

Macbeth must assassinate the future: he remembers too much of it. His imagination is paralysingly proleptic. He is an inverse image of Funes the Memorious in the Borges story. The latter is so crammed with the memorialized detail of the present and the past that he is disqualified from the daily functionings of life. Memory is all, and its weight is monolithic. The grammar of Macbeth's imagination leads so ineluctably towards the future, the tomorrow and tomorrow and tomorrow, that he must either slide into madness, or take up his sword and become time's avenger, even before time has made its lethal deliveries. The memory of the future darkens Macbeth's soul until there is no light to be had anywhere; his wife's memory of the past inhabits the darkness that should bring her sleep. What connects them both is murder. And we recall that Macbeth announces that he murders sleep, and not simply his own.

The ultimate logic of secrecy is that your own mind becomes a prison. Now Lady Macbeth is a highly methodical woman. When she cries, 'Out damned spot', she is issuing commands even in her sleep. And such commands obey the requirements of economy in the old sense: actions pertaining to household management. So she is hygienically commandeering, even as a somnambulist. They must all scrub and scrub until the stains of sin should disappear. But the stains remain, imprinted too indelibly on the surface of her mind. When she is locked in sleep, she cannot escape the graffiti on those dark walls. They are written in Duncan's blood. And she had not expected the old man to have so much of it.

The Doctor here is remarkably enlightened, simply by knowing his limitations. Most doctors around at the time — Simon Forman, for example — would have reached for the almanac, to cast a horoscope. See what astral influences might be contending here. But this one can see that contemporary medicine should commit no trespass, where it possesses no gifts of analysis and repair. 'This disease is beyond my practice,' he says. And he also gives a diagnosis: 'More needs she the divine than the physician.'

Medicine was in a state of radical flux. Astrology was still being used, but was being edged out. Its greatest put-down is Edmund's speech at the beginning of *Lear* – a magnificent dismissal of cosmological nonsense as potent now as it was then. It was in 1518 that the College of Physicians had been founded. That might have been a step in the right direction but then in 1564 John Dee had been appointed the royal adviser in mystic secrets. He had embroiled himself in trouble for casting the Queen's horoscope. He spent his life trying to transmute base metals into gold, and communicate with spirits in the regions beyond, always in the hours of darkness. He might have been the finest mathematician in Europe. These were complicated times. There was still an inheritance from Galen, which was in the process of being discredited during Shakespeare's lifetime. The Humours: sanguinary, phlegmatic, choleric and melancholic. The space between the physician and the quack was often minuscule. Panaceas could be sought in arcane books, like the ones on Dee's shelves; they could also be bought in boxes and jars. So it shows a remarkable lack of presumption on the Doctor's part that he gazes on a troubled spirit and declares himself incompetent. Her ladyship's condition is of a sort that can't be cured with a Jacobean aspirin.

MACBETH INSTRUCTS THE Doctor as to what precisely he wants — he wants a cure for dysnarrativia. He wants the old world to be re-assembled, the old tale re-told. In any case, by this stage of the play he appears to think of conscience as little more than a womanish complaint. And it is of course a relatively recent addition to Lady Macbeth's psyche:

> Canst thou not minister to a mind diseas'd
> Pluck from the memory a rooted sorrow,
> Raze out the written troubles of the brain,
> And with some sweet oblivious antidote
> Cleanse the stuff'd bosom of that perilous stuff
> Which weighs upon the heart?

We are still having a go at this, of course. And we are equally unsuccessful, even though we have substituted Fentanyl for poppy and mandragora. The grief of what you have done, what you have irreversibly done, is an unhealing wound.

Lady Macbeth helps to forge the grammar of her own life; she then finds its manacles inescapable. We are entitled to think that Macbeth and his wife entertained the fancy of being king and queen; perhaps even entertained the possibility of killing to achieve the throne. But to entertain a wish is neither to pursue nor to fulfil it. It is only when Duncan comes unexpectedly under their roof that the possibility of fulfilment arises. Macbeth immediately backs off; his wife immediately presses forward.

OUTSIDE THE REALM OF HUMAN UNDERSTANDING.

'I AM THAT I am', says Yahweh in Exodus, or 'I will be who I will be', since Hebrew has no present tense for the verb to be. This verbal phrase refuses the ranks of serried nouns all round it; it will not be nominally contained. Moses is hunting for description and definition, so that he might carry them back to his people, like epistemological souvenirs, but he is given instead a formula for unlimited dynamism. Aquinas would later ponder whether the word 'God' should really be a verb. Subsequent scholars have argued that *theos* derives ultimately from the Sanskrit *di*, to gleam.

'What god are you?' is not a functional question when addressed to Yahweh. To ask it means you are in the wrong language game.

This is a dysnarrativia between the language of God and the language of humanity; we might even say, the grammar of the human and the grammar of the divine. The linguistic structure of being in both is disjunct and unassimilable. 'What god are you?' is not a functional question when addressed to Yahweh. To ask it means you are in the wrong language game. You are trying to pluralise the indivisible. Faced with such a consuming light, you cannot shade your eyes with taxonomy. *Ehyeh asher ehyeh*, says the Lord. I am not designed to fit into the Israelites' linguistic containers. Those containers will have to fracture and break even to approach me. Do not translate me into language that can never contain me, says Yahweh. This burning bush you see before you leaves no traces.

This is a revelation of light. In *Macbeth* we have revelations of darkness. When Macbeth asks the Weird Sisters what they are doing, and they reply, A deed without a name, they are effectively saying what Sweeney says in T. S. Eliot's 'Agon:' 'I've gotta use words when I talk to you.' You are in one world of meaning, and I am in another entirely. Between the two lies the realm of dysnarrativia; the linguistic no-man's land. Signifying nothing.

IS THIS THE PROMISED END?

ON LOSING HIS only son to the Plague — King Pest as he called it — Simon Forman wrote:

> Darkness was on the face of the Deep,
> Darkness without light,
> Darkness in speaking,
> Darkness in understanding.

This contemporary of Shakespeare could be standing in for Edgar in *King Lear*. The catastrophic events contrived by his half-brother Edmund have landed him in serious trouble. Should he continue to be his courtier self then he will be at the least imprisoned and possibly executed. So he undergoes the most radical transformation conceivable: this bejewelled child of the Court becomes a Bedlam beggar, naked and chanting a lingo from the darkness of the madhouse. How the dim-witted and urbane courtier suddenly finds this phenomenal linguistic resource Shakespeare never reveals. Edgar's linguistic survival-kit renders him a freak of apocalyptic prophecy and metaphysical provocation. His darkness in speaking alerts us to how dark the age has become. The only light we can find must be within that darkness. There is a precursor for this in the opening of John's gospel: 'And the light shineth in darkness; and the darkness comprehended it not.' Like the poetry of Paul Celan, Edgar's speeches wring the language dry. This feels like the ultimate grammar and lexicon of dysnarrativia. Except of course that this dysnarrativia is willed; it is verbal camouflage.

It is willed then, but under duress. Edgar trawls the depths of language to avoid losing his life on the surface. The surface is the most dangerous plane: that is where you are visible and audible. That is where people imagine they understand you; their classifications follow. Classification often precedes punishment, and punishment might well be death. Edgar on the Heath is beyond the law. The grand prefect of the law is here, but he has shed his clothes and, it would seem, his wits along with them.

Edgar as Mad Tom comes close to glossolalia. His language is accessing sources entirely closed to the courtier he was such a short time back. We know some of the sources are from Samuel Harsnett's denunciation of papish impostures. Hardly Edgar's palace reading, surely? He would have been more likely to have had his head in Castiglione. But he impersonates with panache:

> The foul fiend haunts poor Tom in the voice of a nightingale. Hoppedance cries in Tom's belly for two white herring. Croak not, black angel; I have no food for thee.

Perhaps as radical is Lear's catastrophic fall from his previous narrative into a tale seemingly told by an idiot, and most notably glossed by the Fool. We are so used to the play that we don't always register just how hideous is Lear's curse upon Goneril:

> Into her womb convey sterility!
> Dry up in her the organs of increase,
> And from her derogate body never spring
> A babe to honour her!

In Elizabethan and Jacobean terms, sterility is the cancellation of the future for this particular individual or family. But see how close to the surface this language was (we are still in Act One).

However confident we might be in our narratives, dysnarrativia is never more than a curse or two away.

WILLED DYSNARRATIVIA.

DYSNARRATIVIA IS NORMALLY thought of as involuntary. Damage to the neurophysiological machinery or a radical imbalance between psyche and world distort or occlude the language of the user. In Jakobson's classic essay on metaphor and metonymy, he studied how stroke victims often suffered a swerving of linguistic use either towards the metaphoric or the metonymic mode.

But what happens if your dysnarrativia is willed? What kind of language are we looking at if the subject deliberately disconnects from communal usage and expectation, for whatever reason? Hamlet does just this. After his solitary encounter with the Ghost, he speaks in a riddling manner: his communications are of a sort that thwart expectations. Marcellus and Horatio are desperate to discover what secret knowledge, what longed-for gnosis, the Ghost has bequeathed to the Prince. And Hamlet finally reveals it:

> There's ne'er a villain dwelling in all Denmark
> But he's an arrant knave.

Horatio is astounded by the banality of this and says so:

> There needs no ghost, my lord, come from the grave
> To tell us this.

Why has Hamlet reverted to proverb and cliché to provide his answer? Is this a form of defence or equivocation? Is it possible that, full of the appalling revelation the Ghost has delivered, Hamlet decides to dissimulate there and then? If he speaks truthfully, he may be considered mad. His dissimulating manner will soon have him classified as mad in any case. And that appears to suit him. Dysnarrativia can at least supply an alibi.

Subsequently, Ophelia has her wits battered askew by her father's death. She had already been traumatized by her princely lover's rejection, and her father acting as a spymaster, using his only daughter as the spy. Her dysnarrativia is a collapse into earlier forms of language, songs from childhood, bawdy verses. On a mescaline trip in 1934, Walter Benjamin free-associated and found himself writing down the words of lullabies. He and Ophelia were at this moment attuned. Language has lost its referentiality, except in regard to dream and memory. And pain, of course. That leaves traces too ineradicable to erase.

We are entitled to ask what memory traces were there, ineradicably there, in the audience? Within living memory a king had married his brother's wife, precipitating the Reformation in England when he sought to discredit his own betrothal by biblical proofs. How dark and silent a memory might that have been? Hamlet has an inner life; the outer life of the court ceaselessly attacks it. He is mournful, draped in black, still pondering his father's death. But Elsinore is carnivalesque; it is a place of unceasing revels. You can even hear the sound of them out on the battlements. The King carouses. He would appear to have a bellyful of wine night and day. And the Queen undoubtedly enjoys his jocund company. So snugly do they fit together that one can't help wondering if this relationship might not have got started before King Hamlet's death. The old fellow was always away a lot on matters of state, after all. And those Danish winter nights can get seriously chilly.

For some unstated reason, Claudius has never married. Maybe, in one respect, he never needed to. So now the world cries, Rejoice. But Hamlet doesn't feel like rejoicing. Mourning and melancholia engulf him like a massive funeral cloak.

Hamlet inhabits his own persona of insanity the way a man might inhabit irony

He inhabits his own persona of insanity the way a man might inhabit irony; and his comments are ironic frequently enough. When that irony is exhausted he suffers from adjectival overload:

> I should have fatted all the region kites
> With this slave's offal; bloody, bawdy villain!
> Remorseless, treacherous, lecherous, kindless villain!

If only words could kill. But instead, the Prince manœuvres his way through the labyrinth of his own enquiring and distrustful mind. He sees off his old chums Rosenkrantz and Guildenstern before they had the chance to see him off, with the aid of the King of England. He kills his lover's father. He sees his lover's funeral, having helped to drive her wits astray. He sees his mother poisoned by his murderous uncle, now her doting spouse, and finally gets to kill the avuncular assassin himself. The rest is silence; language it seems cannot cope.

DYSNARRATIVIA?

BOTTOM SUFFERS A most peculiar form of dysnarrativia: he switches species. His language is still there, but it becomes no more than the means of enumerating a catalogue of appetities:

> Monsieur Cobweb, good monsieur, get your weapons in your hand, and kill me a red-hipped humble-bee on the top of a thistle; and, good monsieur, bring me the honey-bag.

A posse of obedient fairies is a handy thing if you have been transmuted, and Bottom treats them all like preternatural waiters, for he has been translated and so have his earthly appetites. That means, of course, that his language has metamorphosed too. He now inhabits his own words as though they were the guide book to an enchanted forest, with a sizeable menu attached. And as for Lavinia in *Titus Andronicus*, she suffers the most tragic form of dysnarrativia: her tongue is cut out and her hands are cut off. Not only is she denied the vocalizations of language; the silent realm of semiology is denied her too. As Chiron from the grandeur of his grubby power proclaims: 'Nay, then I'll stop your mouth.'

The line between dysnarrativia and impersonation is a wavering one. If I can no longer tell the story of myself, at the risk of my life, then I must tell the story of someone else instead, and become that someone in the telling. Rosalind butches it up as Ganymede, in order to train Orlando to be a man; an acceptable one. He turns out to be a zealous student. Portia dons not only manhood but a judge's robes. She then proceeds to administer justice in a most ingenious manner: she quibbles over the wording of the legalities.

Some at the time might have thought this womanish. It worked, all the same. Mariana in *Measure for Measure* has to pretend to be a reluctantly yielding nun, in order to win back her beloved Angelo. This is an exercise of the bed-trick. As William Empson pointed out, it was based on the Elizabethan notion that all women are interchangeable after twilight. It goes back a long way before Elizabeth's reign. The same trick was pulled between Jacob, Rachel and Leah in Genesis. There is probably a vague theology behind it: if God had meant us to recognise one another's individual features in the hours of intimacy, he would not have switched the lights out.

But Hamlet's father is dead, surely the most fatal form of dysnarrativia? Even so, he carries on speaking. Except that he is only heard in the echo-chamber of his son's mind. Dysnarrativia, whatever else it might be, can be a form of enforced solitude. Or, in the case of Caliban, a non-linguistic creature is blessed with human language. Except that he now says the apparent blessing is no more than a curse, since all it has truly taught him is *how* to curse. It is not merely a question then of whether or not we can competently tell the story of ourselves. It is also a question of who owns the language in which we tell the tale. And what precisely is the place of our narrative in that linguistic hierarchy?

6.

Considering *I*, alone

THE LAW OF THE FIRST PERSON:

'Little i will need to go from minuscule to majuscule if it is ever to stand on the shoulders of giants and begin to glimpse the horizon.'

COLERIDGE PUT THE matter thus:

My opinion is this: that deep thinking is attainable only by a man of deep feeling, and all truth is a species of revelation…It is *insolent* to *differ* from the public *opinion* in *opinion*, if it be only *opinion*. It is sticking up little *i by itself*, *i* against the whole alphabet. But one *word* with *meaning* in it is worth the whole alphabet together. Such is a sound argument, an incontrovertible fact.

We know of course that there can be no one word with meaning in it without a host of others signifying a myriad significations all around it, but Coleridge's point is still a sound one. Raising the little *i* by itself, purely to set one disputatious opinion against others, is simply intellectual insolence. If you wish to counter scholarship, or even mere custom, you will need something stronger than 'opinion' with which to effect the contradiction. Intellectual democracy is not a matter of statistics; authority is required if a given position is ever to be made tenable.

Coleridge's 'little *i*' might not have grown any bigger since his time, but it has certainly not grown less in number. Its programmatic assumption is that any serious change in intellectual position might take the form of a glissade, whereas it is in fact always an arduous ascent. Or perhaps an arduous descent. Either way, a cost will be involved for the climber. Modern physics teaches us that no change of position is ever possible without an exchange of energies. Little *i* will need to go from minuscule to majuscule if it is ever to stand on the shoulders of giants and begin to glimpse the horizon.

CONSTRUCTING AND DECONSTRUCTING THE EGO.

SO WHAT IS the *I* anyway, whether upper or lower case? What does it mean to speak in the first person after Freud? How commanding is that majuscule pronoun? And how many little *i*'s are in truth swarming inside it, like ants in an anthill, but without the instinctive imperative that keeps every one of those ants in line and on-message? If Freud's work can still be taken to signify anything other than an over-ambitious modern mythopoeia, then what might we derive from it? That the ego, which asserts supremacy in order to beguile itself on through the tunnel of its survival, is in truth just as often subject to the forces it strives to command as master of the same. That the forces swarming in the unconscious are not tameable by diktats issuing from the ego; that the ego might be the seat of rational and conscious consideration, but that other entangled forces in the psyche can still conduct a civil war which renders the kingdom of that psyche at best a divided one, and at worst a scene of perennial devastation.

What does it mean to speak in the first person after Freud? How commanding is that majuscule pronoun?

The notion that the *I*, whether big or little, did not utter itself as a tranquil psychic unity would have come as no surprise to William Blake. *I*, he knew only too well, was one mode of expression for a congeries of disputing and even warring energies and forces, sometimes of transcendent, even demonic, power. As those forces reconfigure (or reconsider) themselves, the nature of the *I* inevitably changes too. He put the matter punningly in 'The Mental Traveller': 'For the Eye altering alters all.' What we see is how we see; and how we see is who we are. In 'Auguries of Innocence' in the Pickering Manuscript, Blake makes the crucial distinction between seeing with the eyes and seeing through them. Those who see with the eyes merely see through conventions; they see what is translated through a species of collective egotism, a vast collective lens of received opinion. To see through the eyes, though, is not merely to confront the seeable with the dictates of your little *i*, but instead to permit the seeable to make its presence felt to the watcher. It is to allow oneself to be penetrated. It is, in Blake's usage from *The Marriage of Heaven and Hell*, to attend as the doors of perception are cleansed. You cannot interpret meaningfully if you start from the proposition and the pre-position that you already know. Blake's home off the Strand was called by intimates like Palmer the House of the Interpreter. Here was one whose host of little *i*'s had been transcended. Here was one whose thoughts were not traded as counters in the marketplace of opinion.

Truth is a species of revelation. It requires intelligent appreciation of the subject to be explored, together with skill in rendering the perceptions into form.

'All truth is a species of revelation.' In other words, it is not an opinionated imposition upon the scheme of things, but a detection of the nature of things effected by intelligent and scrupulous attentiveness. Now this was also Ludwig Wittgenstein's understanding at the time that he was writing the *Tractatus*: insofar as language could convey truth at all, then it embodied something of the nature of the relations between things. If I say, the moon orbits the earth, then my statement, by a parallelism of form, by means of formal sympathy, must convey a reality to be perceived in nature. Truth is a species of revelation. It requires intelligent appreciation of the subject to be explored, together with skill in rendering the perceptions into form. In terms of language, this is what we normally call the ability to write. That ability, in its greatest scope, Coleridge would have added, is not mechanical but imaginative; not so much mimetic as esemplastic.

In coining the term *'esemplastic'*, Coleridge was trying to fathom something about the working of the human mind: how, confronted with the many, it invariably sets about searching out the one from which the many must originally spring. There is a hyponymic urge in us which makes thought possible: seeing a vast variety of green growths, we say *grass*; seeing a vast variety of atmospheric conditions, we say *weather*; seeing a vast number of creatures with certain similarities, we say *species*. The urge can enlighten us, but it can mislead us too. We held for thousands of years that the Pentateuch was written by one man, Moses, and that the Psalms were written by one man, David. We put together a variety of heterogeneous texts and called it the Bible. Some insist that that vast heterogeneity of texts had only the one author too, as well as the singular title. Faced with the unimaginable vastness of the cosmos we insist it all originated at a single point, indeed a singularity: the Big Bang. And everything, on our present calculations, is ultimately made of protons, neutrons and electrons, unless dark matter reveals some material as yet entirely unexpected.

This is not, Coleridge would point out, the urge for simplification (though it can be that); it is the urge for clarification and comprehensibility. If reality were to present itself as no more than an infinite array of forces and forms, then we would be condemned to live in an unceasing perceptual flux. Intellection requires hierarchic subjugation, taxonomy, hyponymy. We search for the structure of things, even if that should contradict our previous ontologies. When we found in the 1890s that the atom had a structure, we contradicted the ontology built into our own treasured etymology. *'A-tomos'* meant indivisible; but that which has a structure *is* divisible. Our own words had been deceiving us.

But our own words might also put us right; so Freud believed anyway. Parapraxes are a correction of the conscious part of us by the less conscious. Parapraxes in their verbal form permit genuine desire to invade the channels of censorship and propriety. A Buck's Fizz proffered by the man in the suit, who is growing squiffy, becomes a Fuck's Bizz, because that's his real preoccupation, which inhibition precludes him from saying consciously, but the repressed returns and mangles his locution, aided by an alcoholic lubricant. And so Freud comes to believe that all emotion, all desire, and the repression of the same, can be compressed into a single triangulation: between id, ego and superego. These are the quarks and electrons of our psychic life. These are the rudiments out of which everything else is constructed. Parapraxes alter the *I* (and thereby the eye) by forcing it to own up to conflicts within itself which it would sooner hide. Properly understood they might even force us to see through the eye rather than with it. That is, if you believe that the practice of free association, when processed through the analytic procedures of a Freudian practitioner, can connect up the disparate contingencies into an overall causality.

THE I OF POIESIS

THE POETIC *I* occupies a special space. What Roman Jakobson calls the poetic function permits the written word within the written space to float relatively free of referentiality; to foreground the gestures of its own linguistic play, its fictionality. Here is an *I* that can own up to containing any number of little *i*'s, without necessarily diminishing its stature. 'I contain multitudes', Whitman informs us (each presumably with its own *i*), and if that appears to threaten the protocols of coherence, then so be it: 'You say that

I contradict myself. Very well. I contradict myself.' The logical distance between *I* and '*myself*' means that I can at least split my identity into the nominative and the accusative. I can treat myself simultaneously as subject and object. In this act of knowing myself knowing, of apperception, I am owning up to the fact that the *I* is not self-enclosed and homogeneous. Like the atom, it turns out to have a structure after all, and is therefore divisible.

At least as heroic as Whitman's poetic *I* was Mayakovsky's. The Russian poet insisted that his own ego had dissolved into the great historic force of the revolutionary masses. In '150 Million' he writes: '150, 000, 000 speak through my lips.' And then we had the recurrent *I* of Robert Lowell's poetry, in and out of madness, in and out of jail, in and out of the hospital, and yet this *I* can never be dissevered from those other nominal agents of New England, the patrician Lowells. This is an *I* of enhanced genealogy, however desperate its battles with the Republic, even when it disintegrates before us.

In Molly's soliloquy at the end of *Ulysses*, there are only eight sentences, and hardly any punctuation. Majuscules are retained only for names and her own personal pronoun, the *I*. Molly, even as she dozes off, still holds on to the big *I* against the little one. She is still insisting that she remain in command of her narrative, her little boat. If she cannot be captain, precisely, then she will at least sail on as Pirate Jenny. By the time we reach *Finnegans Wake* the *I* is no longer singular; it has become a multitude, and the language is shaping any *I* as much as that *I* can ever shape the language. This was to be Lacan's message later, and that thinker was greatly preoccupied with *Finnegans Wake*, a book which contains the remark:

'I have something inside of me talking to myself.' There are at least three translatable *I*'s in that sentence.

But both Joyce and Lacan had been anticipated by Rimbaud. Rimbaud understood that he was fashioned by the language, and that the force of that fashioning was strong enough to sever signifier from signified, while still keeping a poetic structure intact. This is precisely what happens in 'Le Bateau Ivre', where the poem's stanzaic and prosodic structure is the only principle of order that survives, along with grammar. Jakobson often talks in his work of how poetry, in its rhythmic and aural structurings, its formalities and repetitions, can provide a principle of textual coherence which in other types of writing would have to be provided by narrative or discursive unities. Rimbaud understands this, and he also understands the principle of the formulation: *Je est un autre*. The key word here is *est*; had it been *suis*, as it was in Gérard de Nerval's '*Je suis l'autre*', then the rupture could be mild, indeed negotiable. But if the first person can be transposed into the third with only a single empty space between them, then, as Othello put it, chaos is come again.

In his early *Economic and Philosophical Manuscripts*, Marx spoke freely of alienation. We, as a species, have become alienated from ourselves. The division of labour and the control of the means of production by those owners who receive the benefits of the surplus value created by industrial production, mean that the maintenance of our means of subsistence actually thwarts our appetite for meaning, turns us into agents of our own semantic dislocation. The whole of the alienated system expresses itself in the ultimate runic device of capitalism: the commodity.

And when Freud began his practice he was known as an alienist; one who could enter the alienated realm of the mentally disturbed and translate the mangled language to be heard therein into the coherence of scientific explanation. Freud was explicit: he sought to translate id into ego, so that we might journey from the inchoate and irrational to the realm of the rational and self-comprehending. Rimbaud's programme was the precise opposite. He would seek the *'dérèglement de tous les sens'*. Not merely the derangement of the senses, but their deregulation. One might translate his wish thus, as a precise inversion of Freud's programme: to translate ego into id. Between these two *I*'s, poetry still ventures. In the *Adagia*, Wallace Stevens reflects that in poetry one wants the imagination to outrun the intellect, if only just. And imagination and intellect remain two aspects of the one *I*, Siamese twins who have grown old enough to argue. Or as we remember the multivocal and translingual text of *Finnegans Wake* putting it: 'I have something inside of me talking to myself.'

The ionic column of the *I* sometimes puts headphones on, in the form of inverted commas, and becomes '*I*', in an effort to block out the sound of the collapsing building of which it was once an ornament.

7.

Looking back in anger

THE PAINTER R. B. KITAJ took his own life in 2007. He was unwell and had decided to have done with things there and then. In any case, the love of his life, Sandra Fisher, had died more than a decade before. His late paintings seem to indicate that he was keen to join her; many of them are in the form of angels, highly eroticized angels, quite a few bearing the features of himself and his dead wife reaching out to one another in a longing strong enough to overcome death.

These paintings are far from being the best of Kitaj, and yet they raise what we might call one of the perennial questions of modernity: what is the relationship between the sacred and the profane, and what ground, if any, might they share? The question was addressed with characteristic vigour by Paul Gauguin in his painting *The Vision after the Sermon*. There Jacob wrestles with his angel, while nuns look on, but it is the nuns who are foregrounded, their drooping winged bonnets much larger than the wings of the angel himself. The priest who has given the sermon is there too, and bears a striking resemblance to the artist. So our visions arise out of us, and are projected on to the profane ground across which we walk, and over which we fight our battles. The sacred is not a different spiritual region to the profane; it is an alternative dimension of the same. We don't go somewhere else to be spiritual; instead we stay where we are and look harder at what we sometimes call the facts that have been set before us.

Kitaj was obsessed all his life with Cézanne, and Cézanne certainly believed that everything needed in life and art was here, right before us, but we had to learn to see with utter integrity, and that meant ridding ourselves of false visual conventions. It is not the subject-matter of art that makes it lofty, but its method of perception. That is why Cézanne wanted to paint a carrot that was pregnant with revolution. It is why he believed the portrayal of a single apple could carry as much transcendent significance as a visual account of the crucifixion. It is why his studies of Mont Sainte Victoire are fuller of necessary information than any photograph has ever been. They have worked harder to arrive at a visual truth. There is more layering here than the Cyclops of a camera lens can ever manage.

One of the striking features of modern art is that it frequently does not look 'finished' in the way of the post-Renaissance art that preceded it. It can seem provisional, even sketchy. There are precedents for this. Rembrandt grew less and less interested in finishing canvases as he grew older. One of his clients, having paid a hefty sum, sent the painting back and asked if the painter would mind finishing it. We see in some of the self-portraits how, having achieved his work on the central features, Rembrandt has no interest left for working on the hands at the margins. A brief diagram would have to do.

If Cézanne had become Kitaj's artistic exemplar at the end of his life, he had been Picasso's at the beginning of his. That difficult man, clambering off each day into the countryside at Arles or into his studio, was fumbling about, trying to discover the contours of modern art — a topography he was constructing, even in the moments of discovering it. 'He didn't know what he was doing,' his widow said to the young disciples who turned up in 1906 to honour his memory. 'You must understand: he didn't know how to finish a painting.'

Not knowing how to finish a painting, or a book: this might not be a bad description of the modernist enterprise.

Not knowing how to finish a painting, or a book: this might not be a bad description of the modernist enterprise. Kafka's writings (and Kafka was crucially important for Kitaj) explore their own state of radical incompletion. In many of Kitaj's paintings the canvas showed through in sundry places to the end. But for those in Paris, who filled the salons and review pages, and knew only too well how to 'finish a painting', Cézanne was filled with contempt. He snarled. Flaubert was filled with the same contempt, and said so repeatedly, also frequently snarling, for the writers in Paris. Art at its most probing refuses the immediate fashions that garner praise.

In his exuberantly eccentric *Second Diasporist Manifesto*, Kitaj wrote: '"He who thinks that he has finished is finished." — The Kotzker; never stop studying, and painting what Cézanne called "studies" and "researches." UNFINISH, in the studio of an old isolate, beyond Art if possible, toward UNFINISHed life.'[1] 'The Kotzker' here was Menahem Mendl of Kotz, the 'Kotzker Rebbe', another troublesome Jew. And 'finish' here, as an act of facile closure, seems to be, in effect, a state of intellectual bad faith. It is that act of completion which cuts off the source of questioning, the motivation of research, the imbalance in the question which perennially needs adjusting (and yet never can be, finally). And we have a curious prolepsis of this condition in William Blake. In his brief and unhappy time at the Royal Academy School, the young unteachable ranted at the eminent Keeper, Moser: 'These things that you call Finish'd are not even Begun; how can they then be Finish'd? The man who does not know the Beginning never can know the end of Art.'

KITAJ. THAT OLD isolate in his studio is presented to us here, in all his spiritual experimentalism, and his earthly passions. He was a curmudgeon. And for once Samuel Johnson's spurious etymology in his *Dictionary of the English Language* of 1755 seems appropriate: a *coeur méchant*, or wicked heart. This posthumously published autobiography can at times still manage to shock. Kitaj went in search of whores all his life (except at the end), and celebrated them in his art.

Here he reveals that neither his relationship with his Princess, Sandra Fisher, nor his marriage to her, stopped this particular quest. When they lived in Paris, Sandra would occasionally accompany him on the harlot trail. If the modern world has a way of coping with such behaviour, except in outright condemnation, it has not recently revealed it.

In anthropological terms, the canvas is a sacred space in its own right. What applies within its boundaries does not apply beyond them; it has that in common with the nave of a church, or a football pitch. That sacred space was where Kitaj chose to live for much of his life. His stated ambition was to draw better than any Jew who had ever lived. His engagement with modernism was life-long, but then so was his commitment to figurative art. He still believed that the easel painting was a revolutionary space, which had not been superseded by either installations or Duchampian ready-mades, though he loved Duchamp. Inside the sacred space of the canvas the struggle could continue, as Keats put it, 'Betwixt Damnation and Impassion'd clay'. That the canvas becomes the designated area of negotiation between the sacred and the profane can be seen as one aspect of its 'unfinishability'. What is going on here transcends any neat categories of ocular compartmentalization. It returns endlessly to that inexhaustible subject, the human clay.

An American living in London, a remarkably gifted draughtsman pursuing an obsession with the modernist heritage, Kitaj was also obsessively Jewish. As the first sentence of his *Diasporist Manifesto* puts it: 'I have Jew on the brain.' He tried to encourage others to join him in a modern, self-consciously Jewish avant-garde. None of his friends or colleagues wanted to know. They preferred to be known as artists who were Jews; not as Jewish artists. But Kitaj obsessed away, constantly alluding visually to the Holocaust, and saying that the greatest artist of his time, the number one contender for greatness, had undoubtedly been Kafka. Gershom Scholem, another of Kitaj's heroes, believed that Kafka walked the line between mysticism and nihilism, understanding as he did that the tradition of revelation was always in place, but that we no longer had any ready access to it. Modernity had insulated us from the transmissibility of revealed truth. This connects to Walter Benjamin's notion of 'the decay of experience' in modern times. The vastness of our information starts to feel more and more prosthetic. The truth becomes deictic, no longer internalized. We refer to it, but it finds it hard to live or thrive inside us. We might also note of all Kafka characters that the harder they work at their craft or profession, the lonelier they become.

So he liked to quote Einstein: 'I am a profoundly religious non-believer.' Kitaj was obsessively Jewish, in his own idiosyncratic way, but Yahweh seems to have disappeared somewhere between Kafka's boundaries of mysticism and nihilism. Yahweh became like the canvas in some of Cézanne's exercises in *passage*: there as a grounding to be merged into and risen out of, taking its colouring (chameleon-like) from our spiritual combat, the chiaroscuro of our intellectual itinerary. Our delineations of spiritual truth can only be oblique. And here Kitaj might be largely following Scholem. Any god whom we might seek to formulate, the Almighty himself has already transcended. The question is not whether one believes in God, but whether one can accede to or acclaim any formulation of 'God' that is intellectually available. In one sense, all studies of religion finally come down to questions of philology. Any manifestation of God in art or theology can only ever glancingly touch that kabbalistic *Ein-sof*, which is the infinite power. The Lord might utter himself forth as *sefirot*, or emanations, but an emanation is neither a definition nor a portrait. All we can ever discover are traces, either in a text or within the sacred space of the canvas. A mystery explained is a mystery betrayed or exploded. You are permitted to provide a commentary, even a critique, but never an explanation. All philology ultimately approaches 'the word of God', the way Nicodemus approached in the dark to find out what these seemingly salvific words might actually mean.

Kitaj was a visual artist in an age of fragmentation, and he never forgot the fact. The classic artistic response to fragmentation is montage. The advantage of montage is a universal allusiveness not just to one tradition, but to all of them simultaneously. Its danger is a slick eclecticism. At the height of his powers, in a painting like *The Hispanist*, Kitaj seemed able to recapture the vividness of the pictorial portrait at its greatest, together with an acknowledgment that the canvas had flattened, that after Cézanne the table would always tip forward into the plane of its own composition. And that after Picasso, the sacred space of the canvas was now open to suggestion, sometimes from the ancient past. The ancient past offers forms that still elude the present.

Kitaj was also a midrashist. Such an interpreter usually operates in words, but he (word-obsessed as he was) functioned through images. Midrash returns to a canonic text, and asks of it questions it could not ask of itself. It is, in the sense of both Walter Benjamin and Gerhard Scholem, a critique. In their sense, critique is an awakening from textual entrapment. Our textual entrapment is a necessity: it represents our only possibility of freedom, since it provides us with the necessary literacy to understand our labyrinthine situation. Critique never abandons tradition; it puts it into suspension while granting considerable autonomy to the informed intelligence. Kitaj endlessly returned upon history and belief in the spirit of critique. That critique frequently takes the form of montage: lay one image beside another and they silently comment upon one another. Like two integers multiplied, they can produce a third neither left to itself could have predicted.

What new information might the modern midrashist bring to ancient formulations, images and traditions? One of the most radical is dream. It was Surrealism that insisted that the dream presents us with as much relevant data as is provided by the ocular waking information we used to call realism. This is why Walter Benjamin based the method of his *Arcades Project* on Surrealism: the dream was integral to his vision, and the phantasmagoria was society's way of dreaming – often its way of dreaming the age to come. If the dream is as central to modernity as the city plan, then our means of representation are immeasurably enriched and disrupted. This is what the Surrealists understood: the need for commando-raid juxtapositions. Freud was baffled by their efforts. As he told André Breton, he did not understood what Surrealism actually wanted. These characters seemed to be celebrating facts that he could only mourn.

There is a great deal of dreaming in Kitaj's pictures. The dreaming process is central to his way of conceiving compositions. This is evidently the case in a picture like *The Philosopher–Queen* where the female figure bilocates in a progress back to her own dreaming room, or *The Symbolist*, whose somnambulism would surely have struck a chord with Breton. The streets of Surrealism are filled with the contents of bedrooms, including some of the bodies. 'I came out of Surrealism,' Kitaj said. His form of the method lent itself to allegory, since the *trouvaille* always points in two directions. Firstly towards the contingency of its arrival in this space, but secondly to the causality of its manufacture and its embodied meaning.

But many of the larger canvases are also dream-instantiated. *If Not, Not* has T. S. Eliot in the foreground, enticed by a contemporary nymph, while in the background lurks the entrance to Auschwitz-Birkenau. There is a severed head; bodies lie around. This is montage informed and inspired by dream, a dream that is all too often a nightmare, that nightmare of history which Stephen Dedalus was so anxious to awake from. This is one midrashist's take on the hideous goings-on of the twentieth-century. When Kubrick was making *Doctor Strangelove*, it soon struck him with great force that he could not make this simply as a realist film: the category was not flexible enough to contain the insanity to be portrayed. So it became fantastical, comic, satiric and surreal, more Jonathan Swift than George Eliot, and the same process goes on frequently in Kitaj. Montage is one way to convey the sheer incompatibility of so much in life and history that coexists. In *His New Freedom*, Kitaj combines two incommensurable forms of existence in one human figure, as if Caliban and Ariel had miscegenated. They clone themselves into a spiritual bifurcation.

One book that Kitaj was never far away from was the poetry of Emily Dickinson. She is a supreme example of the poet as philologist, worrying away unceasingly at what words actually mean. She talks of her neighbours rising each day, polishing their shoes and addressing an eclipse they call Father. 'Eclipse' could have come from Scholem. We turn any spiritual being into an idol if we imagine we can formulate all the laws concerning it. What, after all, do the words actually mean? The prime nomenclator, Adam, assigned names to the animals and plants as he saw fit. Their propriety lay in the character of their origination. Such a *lingua adamica* guarantees meaning by the mere act of bestowing it. But language in its later historical manifestations is always mangled and corrupt. Etymology is the study of distortion and decay: the dictionary shows us the extent of our corruption. And history shows us the dire corruption of our etymologies, one reason amongst others why the artist must always be *contra mundum*. Hence Kitaj's injunction to himself in the *Manifesto*: 'Withdraw! More than I have already.'

In this respect, Emily Dickinson, the secret kabbalist of Amherst, was there before him. Her philology was not dictionary-bound so much as street-wise; not that she was seen much on the streets of Amherst. But she frisked the words as though they were criminals. The meaning of a word, said Ludwig Wittgenstein, is its use in the language. But sometimes that 'meaning' might need a poem to divest it of its party frock:

> Much Madness is divinest Sense –
> To a discerning Eye –
> Much Sense – the starkest Madness –
> 'Tis the Majority
> In this, as all, prevail –
> Assent – and you are sane –
> Demur – you're straightway dangerous –
> And handled with a Chain –

Kitaj felt this way about the critics who savaged his 1994 exhibition, where the paintings had been accompanied by his own midrashic commentaries. His beloved wife died shortly after, and at first he held those critics responsible for her death. Later, he came to realise that this underestimated her. She had gone, all the same. He longed to follow. He painted his way towards her over the following years, always edging towards the grave. Emily Dickinson had called it 'the white exploit' – that last departure that awaits us all.

So it was that in 2007 a man lay on a couch in America with a plastic bag tied over his head. On the table there was a bottle, filled the day before with tablets. And a quart of Bourbon, half-empty now. He was dead. He was an artist, at times a great one. He died in the city of angels, Los Angeles, driven from London by the vinegar and bile of a number of hireling critics of the Zeitgeist. That and his wife's death. His posthumously published autobiography is as engaging and outrageous as he was, both as man and artist.

RBK 1932-2007
Requiescat

CHAPTER NOTE

1. This essay, with illustrations, was published 23 April 2018, with accompanying illustrations, in *The Fortnightly Review* as a review of *Confessions of an Old Jewish Painter* by R. B. Kitaj, with an introduction by David Hockney (Schirmer/Mosel 2017). Access: https://fortnightlyreview.co.uk/2018/04/kitaj-looking-back-in-anger/.

8.

Modernist poetics

Let observation with extensive view
Survey mankind from China to Peru.

SO WROTE JOHNSON, rendering into English the gist of Juvenal's tenth satire. Coleridge ordered those lines out of their party frock and then re-rendered them thus:

Let observation with extensive observation survey mankind extensively.

Coleridge had called the earlier poet's bluff. Periphrasis and repetition are not a display of poetic development; merely an accretion of 'poetic diction'. As Coleridge called Johnson's bluff, modernist poetics effectively calls tradition's bluff. Off with the metrical outfit, it says, and kindly leave all poetic diction at the door. Put your money where your mouth is, and let's see how much your words are actually worth – that is the modernist ethos. Its vigorous programme of 'making it new' aimed at two things: inclusivity and dynamism. All that was of any worth in the past would have to be included in the present's text, perhaps in severely abbreviated form, but never merely as pastiche. And anything of any relevance in the present had to be included too, interleaved with the past's textuality, including the current language of the street, uttered with full demotic urgency. The sought-for dynamic effect would then be a dialectic between tradition and modernity, as it struggled to find its shifting register in modern usage and modern form.

How is the past rendered modern?

Eliot's criticism of *Le Sacre du Printemps*, which he watched with great interest, was that the ritual content remained entirely in the past. As he wrote in the Dial: 'The Vegetation Rite upon which the ballet is founded remained, in spite of the music, a pageant of primitive culture.'[1] Only the music and choreography were meaningfully of the present. In this, it was unlike Eliot's own use of myth and ritual in *The Waste Land*. Tiresias is not back there then, when he appears in the poem; he is here right now. He watches the mechanical seduction in the bedsit, present in the present moment, just as he once watched the same goings-on in Thebes nearly three millennia before. Unless the present can be brought into full contact with the past in such an interactive and interpretative manner, then the past is little more than a sequence of antiquarian addenda, whether rendered through pastiche or burlesque. Tiresias must leave Thebes and travel through the intervening years, until he arrives in London at the time of the poem's action. This, Eliot felt, was very much what was not happening in Stravinsky's ballet. The virgin dancing herself to death to renew the seasons' fecundity was safe in the museum of her own remoteness. The ritual was unlikely to trouble anyone having breakfast at the Savoy the following morning.

And the same applies to the use of traditional devices, whether poetic or dramaturgical. In *Sweeney Agonistes*, Eliot was struggling to find a way of recreating the chorus for modern times. When Wauchope, Horsfall, Klipstein and Krumpacker chant their lines at the end, the past and the present are equally present:

> When you're alone in the middle of the night and
> you wake in a sweat and a hell of a fright
> When you're alone in the middle of the bed and
> you wake like someone hit you in the head
> You've had a cream of a nightmare dream and
> you've got the hoo-ha's coming to you.
> Hoo hoo hoo.[2]

Here the furies have convincingly travelled from ancient Greece and taken a modern form. The *Oresteia* has discovered a modern way of uttering its terrors and mysteries. Here we see Eliot negotiating the demands of modernity in his verse. A few years later he will begin his long withdrawal from this challenge; he will instead accept the conventions of a dramaturgy, and the decorous versifying to accompany it, that was pre-modernist in both genre and tone. In *Murder in the Cathedral* written seven years later, we read this:

> It is not we alone, it is not the house, it is not the city that is defiled,
> But the world that is wholly foul.

This is the Chorus, made up we are told of 'Women of Canterbury'. No women of Canterbury ever spoke thus, except on Eliot's Canterbury stage, while performing this particular play. No such utterances have ever been heard on Canterbury's actual streets. They have a cathedral there, certainly, but not everyone speaks so ex-cathedratically. This language has moved away fatally from current usage, the authentic sound of people speaking which Eliot had caught so astutely in *The Waste Land*. Sweeney, who had made a brief appearance in that poem, now seems to be dead and buried. There was no further place for that personification of transcendent disruption in Eliot's imagination. And the extraordinary vividness of 'When Lil's husband got demobbed, I said –/ I didn't mince my words, I said to her myself…' has now been abandoned once and for all. Something has gone that will not be returning. And one way of describing what has departed from Eliot's practice is modernist poetics. He has retreated from the front line, where modernism had been fighting its battles. However compelling some of the writing in *Four Quartets* might be, it will never again translate the classics into the language of the street. And this must be registered as a loss, for what we saw in the Chorus in Sweeney Agonistes was modernist poetics thinking itself through (the same was the case with Brecht's contemporary Choruses); the Chorus in *Murder in the Cathedral* is a capitulation to the conventions of full-dress theatre, and the proprieties of versifying that accompany them. These common women, these women of the street, realise that they are now in the theatre, and have thought it better to watch their *p*'s and *q*'s.

THE PRESENCE OF THE PAST.

The past and the present in modernist poetics are like wave and particle in quantum physics: to try to split them is to try split the coin into obverse and reverse. What you are left with is no longer valid currency.

IT IS NOT at all a question of the presence or absence of the past. The past, the modernists say in unison, is simply unavoidable. The question is this: will you permit it to dictate stylistic terms, in which case you will be producing a pastiche, however refined and however convincing, or will you engage in a dialectical engagement with the past, translating it constantly through the language of the present, in order to 'make it new'? David Jones was obsessed all his life by the Arthurian legends; he even translated their ethos and narratives to the trenches in the Great War, where he served as an infantryman and was wounded. He could not abide *Idylls of the King*. He felt that Tennyson had done there what Eliot felt Stravinsky had done in *Le Sacre du Printemps*: left the present in order to occupy the cynosure of the past. This is always an illusory manoeuvre, since the past can only be entered through the present; and — speaking stylistically — the same is true the other way around. It is never either/or; it must always be both/and. The past and the present in modernist poetics are like wave and particle in quantum physics: to try to split them is to try split the coin into obverse and reverse. What you are left with is no longer valid currency.

So we have the opening of *The Cantos*. We do seem to be involved in something close to a pastiche, though an astonishingly vigorous one, vigorous enough in fact for George Steiner to gloss it in his anthology *Homer in English*: 'Clearly one of the very high moments in any anthology of the "Homeric" in the language.'[3] But Pound breaks the surface of his seemingly unproblematic re-entry into the versifying mode of the past:

Lie quiet Divus. I mean, that is Andreas Divus,
In officina Wecheli, 1538, out of Homer.[4]

He is working from a Latin version of the Greek, produced by Andreas Divus. He therefore must acknowledge this. The mode of transmission of the past cannot be ignored in the workings of the modern, since that would amount to a form of illusionism. Had there ever been an equivalent fracture in the surface of *Idylls of the King*, we would have been reading an entirely different poem; one that had entered into a dialectical engagement with Tennyson's present. Any negotiation with the past which merely translates backwards is an evasion, according to modernist poetics. It is Tennyson's evasion of the present which produces lines like this: 'Far liefer had I gird his harness on him.'[5] They did not speak thus then; nor do they speak thus now. The women of Canterbury are beckoning, having been to their elocution lessons.

A CONFUSION OF FAMILIARITIES.

CONSTANTIN BRANCUSI, ONE of the greatest modernists of the visual arts, described the variety of techniques that preceded modernism, many of them highly sophisticated, as 'a confusion of familiarities'.[6] Realist and naturalist techniques became so compelling that, like those legendary grapes painted by Zeuxis, the birds might easily have landed on their two dimensions in search of a proteinaceous meal. And so what? asked modernism. In an age of photography and cinema, why should art only seek to generate a faultless verisimilitude? Why compete where effective competition is pointless (in fact, impossible) anyway? But what then could possibly replace the revered technical aspiration towards faultless verisimilitude? The answer to that was form. In the visual arts and literature, form became paramount. And ancient and legendary forms could now present themselves as a more effective way into modern experience than those more recently polished simulacra of the Victorians and Edwardians. Picasso's discovery of primitive masks or Eliot's use of Sophocles and Aeschylus, or Pound and Joyce's borrowings from Homer – all these were not a retreat from the reality of the present, but a means of finding an accelerated surge into it. Clarity of form permitted an escape from the confusion of familiarities. Picasso visited the paintings of the Upper Palaeolithic, and simply remarked afterwards that the modern artist had created nothing: all the formal power had been present thousands of years before. Centuries of 'realism' had merely served to baffle it. Eliot was fascinated by these paintings too, as forebodings of what modern art was in the process of discovering. Form, it seemed, could connect the present with much earlier times. Aesthetically, it operated as a worm-hole, transcending chronology.

Besides, it had started to occur to some of the modernists that the present had a great deal in common with ancient times, not least in the scale of its unexplained brutality and confusion. The *Oresteia*, that ancient ghost lurking behind the modern text of *Sweeney Agonistes*, explores the dark consequences of the calamities of the Trojan War and the fall of Troy. Eliot was writing in the wake of the greatest mechanized slaughter ever perpetrated, in the trenches of the Great War, and just as Clytemnestra betrayed Agamemnon with Aegisthus, so Eliot's wife had betrayed him with one of his closest friends, Bertrand Russell.[7] If it had been dark then, it appeared to be equally dark now, even though candelabra had been replaced by gas lamps and electric bulbs. And a form must be found in order to contain and convey so much darkness. Such a form can be obtained, Eliot insisted, by employing what he called in his review of *Ulysses* for *The Dial* in 1923, 'the mythical method'.[8] Myth, Freud had decided in *The Interpretation of Dreams*, could supply knowledge unavailable to modern science, in the form of the occulted desires of Oedipus. Those ancient forms we had so recently patronized as bodged attempts at science might turn out, after all, to be the most astute guides to our labyrinthine modern condition. It was time, it seemed, for the more knowing anthropologists to take the boots off their feet and the smiles off their faces. As Wittgenstein furiously scribbled in the margin of his copy of J. G. Frazer: 'This is too big to be a mistake.' Mythic understanding offered a challenge to modern science. Its insights were unhampered by the shallow certainties of positivism.

POUND'S REQUIREMENTS.

EZRA POUND WAS the great pedagogue of literary modernism. He loved spelling things out. Gertrude Stein could evidently have done without quite so much elementary abecedary. As she explains in *The Autobiography of Alice B. Toklas*: 'She said he was a village explainer, excellent if you were a village, but if you were not, not.'[9] All the same, one can be grateful now for the clarity with which he expounded early modernist theory, which is to say, early modernist poetics. He was remarkably lucid in formulating precisely what was required.

What are the resources of verse? In his *ABC of Reading* he enumerated them thus: phanopeai, melopeia, logopeia.[10] Which is to say, imagery, music, and intellectual content; or the denotative and connotative value of words. In 'A Retrospect', he explains that what is needed is a direct presentation of the image, whether it be objective or subjective; the avoidance of any unnecessary words – the minimum linguistic expenditure required to effect the presentation is what is always needed. And finally, the poet is to write according to the necessities of the musical phrase, not according to the dictates of a metronome.[11] It was then, and is now, some of the best advice ever given in regard to the writing of poetry.

But we might note a tendency, which would come to have ever-more significance in the development of modernist poetics. What Pound desiderates tends towards a simultaneous and composite image. Such a kaleidoscopic complexity, presented in an instant, appears as a manifold, never as a sequential narrative. Hence Pound's definition of an image as that which presents 'an intellectual and emotional complex in an instant of time'.[12]

Pound's devotion to the ideogram, derived from his work on Ernest Fenollosa, articulates such image-construction as a visual composite. But any purely linguistic form can never render the matter so pictorially. Alphabetic writing is a form of abstraction into what Walter Benjamin called non-sensuous mimesis. In employing it, we have lost the figured traces of the original representative images. Benjamin himself was insistent that the method of his vast *Arcades Project* had to be visual and not linear.[13] Nodal points of time would express the age through intense moments of visual concentration — whether in photography, painting, etching, architecture, or poetry — and this facilitated an entry into the age, a crashing into the surface of its representational remains, where linearity and narrative would have presented instead a chronicle. The chronicle might well have imagined it contained an ætiology, but its narrative mode was already outdated; already unsuited to the kaleidoscopic whirligig of modernity. It was more in the mode of *Idylls of the King* than *The Waste Land*. It told, slowly, where it needed instead to show with great rapidity.

In short, poetry must present itself, immediately and economically, through images which accrue, not tell the story of itself sequentially through narrative or chronicle. That had been Tennyson's method, and that was why his Arthurian epic stepped back into its world of costume drama, not forward on to the streets of Victorian Britain, though if you made your way to the Court, then the Order of the Garter might well still offer its consolations. But that was another form of costume drama altogether. Montage was a more effective representation of modernity than any seamless narrative, but it constantly risked fragmentation.

The method of modernist poetics, then, is presentational. The metaphors tend to lean towards the visual and musical. The whole becomes a tableau. Baudelaire saw Paris as a series of tableaux, which flipped effortlessly from the present to the past. In 'Le Cygne' he walks through a Paris half-demolished by modern developments and gazes on the widowed Andromache, bereft and inconsolable. Any chronological disjunction is overcome by emblematic congruity. Continuity had to be abandoned, in such a succession of images and image-clusters. Discontinuity now had to be celebrated and exploited, as it was in *Ulysses*, and in the final draft of *The Waste Land*. Dublin, Paris and London each became a palimpsest, an overlay of past and present moments.

SEEKING A WHOLE REPRESENTATION OF THAT WHICH IS NOT A WHOLE.

MODERNISM TENDS TO open up forms. The closure offered by the minor form promises its own satisfactions but it is a retreat (whether conscious or not) from modernist poetics. A. E. Housman's poetic formality could never be shaken and broken by the force of modernity, in the way that Eliot's could.

Poiesis tries to construct a whole world. Where this is impossible in the present, the past might well present itself as an option. Pound was acutely aware of this temptation. As he wrote to Joyce, he found himself asking whether he was not 'perhaps better at digging up corpses of Li Po, or more lately, Sextus Propertius, than in preserving this bitched mess of modernity.'[14] This bitched mess of modernity was hard, if not impossible, to fit into any coherent whole. Coleridge invented the word 'esemplastic' to convey the way in which the imagination finds homologies and analogies, and engages in ceaseless pattern-recognition, in order to shape a whole out of such an array of disparate experiences. His neologism has never caught on, but the perception it expressed is true. It is hard for the shaping imagination to acknowledge that some of the material presented to it is, frankly, unshapable into any meaningful whole. Part of the great achievement of modernist poetics was to acknowledge, in the irregular form of its texts, a heterogeneity too speedy to be choreographed into an entirely coherent shaped whole. The form itself must somehow remain open, fissiparous, and therefore vulnerable to contingency; willingly vulnerable. Should the form retreat to the comfort of closure, it will have to renounce modernist poetics, and engage instead in a poiesis which is to that degree nostalgic. The form will in effect become a formalism, and the poiesis will be to some degree exclusivist. It will retreat to that half of art which Baudelaire in his essay 'The Painter of Modern Life' thought of as the beautiful, the traditional, even the antique; but leave out the other half Baudelaire believed to be equally essential: the modern, the chaotic, the ugly, the speedily inchoate.[15] Poiesis in modernist poetics is trying to find a way to negotiate those elements which resist most strongly the unifying forces of poiesis. The Doctrine of Signatures once saw in every element of nature the emblematic forms of a universally expressible meaning. Baudelaire is trying to restore this way of reading the world in his poem 'Les Correspondances'. And it is this grand symbology which Stephen Dedalus in the Proteus episode of *Ulysses* is attempting to conjure for himself when he muses: 'Signatures of all things I am here to read, seaspawn and seawrack, the nearing tide, that rusty boot.'[16]

Modern science has disenchanted our world of those ceaseless interconnections. It has operated as an anonymous disintegrationist, and so has left the imagination with a world in pieces, like Haussmann's Paris as Baudelaire walked through it at dawn. A world more speedily altering than had ever been previously known. (The new science that calls itself *dromology* points out that ours is the only civilisation that has ever posited a speed as its absolute.[17])

It is this incoherence which the text of *The Waste Land* acknowledges:

Falling towers
Jerusalem Athens Alexandria
Vienna London
Unreal

One of the later modernist poets, George Oppen, acknowledges these same irreconcilable multiplicities, but finds in them a tentative principle of hope:

Obsessed, bewildered

By the shipwreck
Of the singular

We have chosen the meaning
Of being numerous.[18]

That last quotation is from the 1968 sequence poem *Of Being Numerous*, which points out that since we refer to Robinson Crusoe as being 'rescued', we have chosen, and what we have chosen are collective not singular meanings. Such heterogeneities of significance can never be entirely harmonised. Discontinuity is the condition of their survival.

BRIEF HISTORY OF A WORD.

To be modernist is simply to acknowledge the time in which you live; it is to relinquish the comforts of that which expresses itself as stylistic historicism.

IN *NEW BEARINGS in English Poetry*, published in 1930, F. R. Leavis never uses the word 'modernist' once, though Laura Riding and Robert Graves had published *A Survey of Modernist Poetry* three years before. Theirs seems to have been the first use of modernist by writers themselves. Eliot never spoke of modernism, at least not in literary terms. When he used the word, it was in relation to theology. Ezra Pound spoke of 'the movement, of our modern experiment, since 1900', and said that its prize exhibit was *The Waste Land*. The term had been one of polemics for a long time. Swift uses it in *A Tale of a Tub*, to signify those ingrates against the classical tradition who so irritated the writer and his patron Temple, in imagining that modern knowledge could ever (or would ever) equal the wisdom of the ancients. Ruskin appears to use it almost always ironically, to signify the latest thinkers, in opposition as always to their immediate forebears. The Roman Catholic Church came to see modernism as a philosophical emblem of all that was most reprehensible in modern thought. It was, effectively, Higher Criticism translating itself into vividly immoral acts, debunking and demythologizing as it went. Such a mode of analytical enquiry was determined to insist that whatever had been held sacred was not in fact sacred. W. Sanday in *Divine Overruling* in 1920 issued the most convincing reply to this: 'I do not disclaim the name of Modernist.

The name describes justly what I aim at being. I aim at thinking the thoughts and speaking the language of my own day, and yet at the same time keeping all that is essential in the religion of the past.'[23] As in religion, so in verse. Here, to be modernist is simply to acknowledge the time in which you live; it is to relinquish the comforts of that temporal illusion which expresses itself as stylistic historicism: 'Far liefer had I gird his harness on him.' Indeed.

FRAGMENTS IN A FRAGMENTARY WORLD.

"These fragments I have shored against my ruins."

SO WROTE ELIOT at the end of *The Waste Land*. Perceptible modernity presents itself in fragments. This is the condition of a world of universal speed and complexity. It is a world which, in aesthetic terms, must try to hold the past and the present in some kind of synchronous balance; that was the writerly endeavour which Eliot was describing in his essay 'Tradition and the Individual Talent'.

Montage, superimposition, sequences of images presented with maximum linguistic force, employing Pound's three areas of resource: phanopeia, melopeia, logopeia. This is the form most suited to the representation of modernity. It was the form employed by Eliot when he was at his most compelling as a poet, in *The Waste Land*, 'Gerontius' and *Sweeney Agonistes*. What happens in the later plays and in *Four Quartets* is that the self-containment, the symmetric self-composure, of the pre-existing genre usurp the perilous modernist poetics that had preceded them. The borders of the writing cease to be porous. There is not a single section of *Four Quartets* which risks the open-ended vulnerabilities of Eliot's earlier verse. Frequently we can see the tell-tale sign of the poetic *hortus conclusus* of versifying: when the last line dictates all that precedes it, so the rest of the poem ends up merely functioning as a preface:

> The dripping blood our only drink,
> The bloody flesh our only food:
> In spite of which we like to think
> That we are sound, substantial flesh and blood –
> Again, in spite of that, we call this Friday good.

One can see Eliot striving for the startling personification effects of Donne in his later religious verse, but Donne was being shockingly modern in his time; here the verse feels too exhausted to do anything but rehearse its own routines. Four Quartets comes to life most convincingly in the passage where the familiar compound ghost speaks in 'Little Gidding'. That ghost utters its imprecations in sub-Dantescan tercets, the most flexible of verse forms for a poet's manoeuvres.

Yeats is a fascinating case because he starts his career as a pre-modernist, goes through a modernist phase culminating in The Tower, and edges in and out of modernist poetics throughout the 1930s. One can see him retreating to the comforts of earlier predictable forms in poems like 'Three Marching Songs' or 'John Kinsella's Lament for Mrs. Mary Moore', but he still keeps venturing to the edges of contingency in 'Man and the Echo', 'The Circus Animals' Desertion' and 'The Statues'. The form is held but we sense the poet's awareness of the threatening forces surrounding it, eroding its edges. Modernist poetics always writes out of a state of crisis. It never recollects itself in tranquillity.

In our dromological world of speed and fragmentation, the construction of closed poetic forms, which are unthreatened by the surrounding chaos, feels parenthetical, a species of retreat. Throughout his editorship of *The Criterion* Eliot described the aim of the journal as the pursuit of, and the elucidation of, 'the European mind'— though he never owned up to the fact that the European mind was here a desideration rather than an intellectual anchor. However platonic the concept, it could not escape the processes of fragmentation that it deprecated. On the title page of *The Anathemata*, David Jones describes the work as 'fragments of an attempted writing'. His book *The Sleeping Lord* is subtitled *and other fragments*. The first book of *The Cantos* was called (and remained called) 'A Draft of XXX Cantos', and its last book was entitled 'Drafts and Fragments'. Dynamic form here can only occur at isolated moments; it cannot command the whole structure, which remains provisional, sometimes to the point of raggedness. The 'bitched mess of modernity' can never be entirely formalized.

POETIC DICTION AND THE 'POETIC FUNCTION'.

WORDSWORTH'S PROBLEM WITH 'poetic diction' seems simple enough: he had grown exasperated with neo-classical periphrases, poets who talked of Selene's chariot when they meant the moon. So he insisted that poetic diction should be the ordinary language of humanity, heightened in intensity through the act of composition. However problematical this notion might turn out to be, the poetic language of *Lyrical Ballads* was exhilaratingly unpretentious and to the point. It had dispensed with the party frock of poesy. And when Pound worked with Yeats on 'modernizing' the older poet's verse, the struggle was to make the diction and imagery harder, crisper, tougher, less inclined to grow misty and blurred. Words like dim and dove-grey simply had to go.

Modernist poetics constantly risks lexical impropriety in its vivid portrayal of modernity.

In taking his blue pencil to Eliot's *Waste Land* typescript, Pound was also seeking the right way for modernist poetics to express itself in a poem he believed great, but at that point still inchoate, in style as much as anything else. So in the original typescript we have Eliot struggling with the line 'When Lil's husband was coming back out of the Transport Corps…' Pound knew the word that was needed, and he inserted it: 'demobbed'.[26] Now this is a tribute to Pound's astuteness. The OED lists the first recorded use of 'demobbed' as 1919. Pound had kept his ear to the ground. Modernist poetics constantly risks lexical impropriety in its vivid portrayal of modernity. The word 'gashouse' also appears in the poem, its first listed usage in poetry in the OED. One meaning of modernist poetics could be defined thus: a ceaseless questioning of linguistic and poetic proprieties, a constant opening-up of poetic form to the language of the day.

It was Roman Jakobson who described what he called the 'poetic function'. The poetic function permits the play of language, the foregrounding of its devices, in effective separation from any immediate referential function. If one were to demand of all poetic functions that they translate themselves into referential discourse, they would soon cease. The answer to 'Shall I compare thee to a summer's day?' would have to be 'What would be the point of that?'

And the poetic function always to some degree commands what we call poetic diction. This is not necessarily in terms of lexis. The shift can occur in syntax and grammar, often in relation to prosody, stanzaic form and rhyme. The poetic function is constantly putting questions to itself, to which it does not always receive an answer. For example, Jacques in his famous speech in *As You Like It* says:

> All the world's a stage
> And all the men and women merely players.
> They have their exits and their entrances…

The world of referential discourse is entitled to ask how precisely you can have an exit before you have had an entrance. You can't, of course. So why the reversal? We do not possess any of Shakespeare's foul papers, but if we did it is plausible to suppose we might find the line first written as 'They have their entrances and their exits…' and one sees the problem immediately. The pentameter has had its back broken, and an unwanted caesura has suddenly appeared after the word 'entrances'; the iambic metre goes into reverse and the last two feet of the line are now unwanted trochees. No actor would want to deliver that line, so this actor-writer simply reverses the order of the words, and we have 'their exits and their entrances'. The pentameter has now regained its backbone and become entirely regular, but at the price of a certain oddity of usage. Poetic function, in the form of the metre, has won out over normal linguistic usage. And something similar happens with Yeats's 'The Cold Heaven':

> Suddenly I saw the cold and rook-delighting heaven
> That seemed as though ice burned and was but the more ice,
> And thereupon imagination and heart were driven

So wild that every casual thought of that and this
Vanished...[28]

We are being carried along almost too quickly to notice that the phrase in English is not 'that and this', but 'this and that'. Unfortunately, that would not have provided Yeats with the half-rhyme he needed for 'ice', and so once again the poetic function wins out over normal usage, this time for the sake of maintaining a rhyme. And the same happens when Gerard Manley Hopkins writes in 'The Windhover' of 'the achieve of, the mastery of the thing.'[29] Here we expect achieve to be verbal but it has become instead a substantive, so the poetic function once again defeats normal usage; this time in terms of grammar. The same will happen when Hopkins turns the noun 'easter' into a verb. This was a Shakespearian manoeuvre, and the poet had learnt it well.

When we look at the verse of Gerard Manley Hopkins, we see a radical adaptation of linguistic usage to suit the needs of the poetic function. Poetic diction, including syntactic innovation, forces the quality of the language to the foreground. In referential discourse this would seem merely perverse or arcane; in poetry it is renewing. Here apparent archaisms serve the purpose of modernist poetics, by defamiliarizing the language, by cutting through the confusion of familiarities.

SO HOW IS MODERNITY TO BE RENDERED?

CUBISM COULD BE described as the most realistic visual mode of the twentieth century in the arts. If we prefer more convenient realisms, which are not so demanding in their compositional truthfulness, that might be the equivalent of retreating to enclosed forms in poetry, or the return to the unproblematical narratives of premodernist novels. Walter Benjamin might well have insisted that montage rather than linearity should command the order of representations in modernity, but montage as a technique can be very demanding. Even Picasso gave it up, in favour of the elegiac heroism of his neo-classical style, although Braque remained faithful to the difficult and uncompromising principle.

> **The ancient could bring you closer to the realities of the present than the accustomed modes of the immediate past…The past exists as long as the present carries it forward…**

Myth functioned for the modernists as a formal simplification, an avoidance of Brancusi's 'confusion of familiarities'. Myth could bring you closer to the present and its horrors and barbarities than the accustomed techniques of naturalism; it was in the widest possible sense, more realistic. The ancient could bring you closer to the realities of the present than the accustomed modes of the immediate past. But such employments were valid only if the ritualistic, the mythic, the legendary, interacted dynamically with the present; only if the past could be made to acknowledge that it only existed at all within the present. The past exists as long as the present carries it forward in time. That is the meaning of the word 'relevance' in terms of art. And, in poetry, this transporting of the ancient could only happen through language. If Tiresias is to make a convincing appearance in the poem, then the word to describe Lil's husband needs to be 'demobbed'. Its demotic urgency is essential. The apparently analeptic manoeuvre of recovering Tiresias had to be matched by a complete modernity of language. The past can only be effectively recovered through forms that are resoundingly modern.

Poiesis can only be made out of an existing world; we have to deal with what we are given. Carl Sagan used to say: 'If you want to make an apple pie, first create a universe.' And David Jones wrote: 'For men can but proceed from what they know, nor is it for the mind of this flesh to practise poiesis, ex nihilo.' If modernity is what we are presented with, then literary forms that preceded modernity are unlikely to be up to the job, without substantial modification. Like Yeats in 1912, they were in need of modernization. Eliot understood this well enough, in principle:

> We cannot revive old factions
> We cannot restore old policies
> Or follow an antique drum.

But he did follow an antique drum (i.e. poetics) when he wrote 'The wounded surgeon plies the steel'. Gerard Manley Hopkins is rightly regarded as one of the great precursors of modernism in verse because, while inhabiting the sonnet form, he entirely re-fashioned it.[32] He did not force the dynamics of current language into a pre-existing form, but instead drilled through the prior expectations of the form to find radical possibilities for the living language inside it. The form after him can never be the same as the form which he inherited. In the best traditions of modernism, he had made it new.

CHAPTER NOTES.

1. Quoted in Ronald Schuchard, *Eliot's Dark Angel* (Oxford: OUP, 1999), p. 113.

2. T. S. Eliot, *The Complete Poems and Plays of T. S. Eliot* (London: Faber and Faber, 1973), pp.125-126. All further references will be given in the body of the text.

3. *Homer in English*, ed. George Steiner (London: Penguin, 1996), p.238.

4. *ibid*, p. 240.

5. *Tennyson: A Selected Edition*, ed. Christopher Ricks (Harlow: Pearson Longman, 2007), p. 739.

6. See *Constantin Brancusi: The Essence of Things*, ed. Carmen Giménez and Matthew Gale (London: Tate Publishing, 2004); see also my earlier comments in *The Fortnightly* under 'Demotic Ritual'.

7. See Ronald Schuchard, *Eliot's Dark Angel*, already quoted.

8. '*Ulysses*, Order and Myth', *Dial*, lxxv (November, 1923). Quoted in *James Joyce, The Critical Heritage, Vol 1, 1907-27*, ed. Robert H. Deming (London: Routledge, 1970), pp. 268-271.

9. Quoted in Humphrey Carpenter, *A Serious Character: The Life of Ezra Pound* (London: Faber and Faber, 1988), p.400.

10. Ezra Pound, *ABC of Reading* (London: Faber and Faber, 1963).

11. Ezra Pound, *Literary Essays of Ezra Pound*, ed. T. S. Eliot (London: Faber and Faber, 1974), pp. 3-14.

12. *ibid*, p. 4.

13. Walter Benjamin, *The Arcades Project*, trans. Howard Eiland and Kevin McLaughlin (London: Harvard University Press, 1999).

14. Quoted in Humphrey Carpenter, *A Serious Character: The Life of Ezra Pound*, p.338.

15. Charles Baudelaire, 'The Painter of Modern Life', in *The Painter of Modern Life and Other Essays*, trans. and ed. Jonathan Mayne (London: Phaidon, 1964), p. 13.

16. James Joyce, *Ulysses*, ed. Walter Gabler (London: The Bodley Head, 1986), p. 31.

17. The word *dromology*, meaning the science of speed, has not yet made its entry into the OED. It is associated with the name of Paul Virilio.

18. George Oppen, *New Collected Poems*, ed. Michael Davidson (New York: New Directions, 2002), p. 166.

19. F. R. Leavis, *New Bearings in English Poetry* (London: Penguin, 1963).

20. Laura Riding and Robert Graves, *A Survey of Modernist Poetry and A Pamphlet Against Anthologies* (Manchester: Carcanet, 2002).

21. Alan Marshall in 'England and nowhere' in *The Cambridge Companion to T. S. Eliot*, ed. A. David Moody (Cambridge: CUP, 1994), p. 102, is quite wrong here. He talks of Eliot's use of the word in the Commentaries he wrote for *The Criterion* as though he were talking of literature, when he was clearly speaking of recent battles in the church. Modernism was not a term he ever used in regard to literature.

22. *The Letters of Ezra Pound*, 1907-1941, ed. D. D. Paige (London: Faber and Faber, 1951), p. 248.

23. Quoted under the headword *Modernist* in the OED.

24. T. S. Eliot, *Selected Essays* (London: Faber and Faber, 1932), p.13.

25. This is disputed by C. K. Stead in his fascinating *Pound, Yeats, Eliot and the Modernist Movement* (London: Macmillan, 1986). Stead argues that Yeats became a *modern* poet, but never a *modernist* one. This essay sees the greatest poems of Yeats between 1912 and 1939 as modernist in the senses suggested above. Yeats might have clung more firmly to traditional forms than the other great modernists, but he still permitted them to be challenged and invaded by the contingencies of modern life. And in that sense he can be described as a modernist, even if only intermittently. The borders of his verse became porous, under the pressure of modernity, in a way that Housman's never were.

26. T. S. Eliot, *The Waste Land: A Facsimile and Transcript of the Original Drafts Including the Annotations of Ezra Pound*, ed. Valerie Eliot (London: Faber and Faber, 1986), p. 13.

27. See 'Linguistics and Poetics' in Roman Jakobson, *Language in Literature*, ed. Krystyna Pomorska and Stephen Rudy (Harvard: Harvard University Press, 1987), pp. 62-94. See also Linda R. Waugh, 'The Poetic Function and the Nature of Language', in Roman Jakobson, *Verbal Art, Verbal Sign, Verbal Time* (Minneapolis: University of Minnesota Press, 1985), pp.143-168.

28. W. B. Yeats, *Collected Poems* (London: Macmillan, 1961), p. 140.

29. Gerard Manley Hopkins, *Poems*, ed. Robert Bridges and W. H. Gardner (Oxford: OUP, 1949), p. 73.

30. We might find a parallel in the world of architecture. In his home in Lincoln's Inn Fields (subsequently to become the museum named after him), Sir John Soane fixed corbel stones from Westminster Hall to the façade of the building. Although they originate in the fourteenth century, these stones are set into a Portland Stone loggia where Soane's great innovation — incised lines to indicate columns and pilasters — are clearly visible. Modern innovation thus incorporates the past.

The two co-exist in radical and visible discontinuity. The past holds the modern in place; the modern does the same for the past.

31. David Jones, *The Anathemata* (London: Faber and Faber, 1952), p. 79.

32. In the case of 'That Nature is a Heraclitean Fire and of the comfort of the Resurrection' (Hopkins, p. 111) this thrice-caudated sonnet has effectively ceased to be a sonnet at all. Here the poet has not so much explored the form as exploded it. Great writing often starts with exploration, even imitation, only to end with transcendence.

9.

Ludwig Wittgenstein

PHILOSOPHY AS MENTAL ENGINEERING

Portraits of Wittgenstein
Volumes I and II

F. A. Flowers III and Ian Ground, editors.
Bloomsbury 2016

LUDWIG WITTGENSTEIN WAS born into a fabulously rich Viennese family. A blessing or a curse? This depends not only on your view of Wittgenstein, but also on your view of riches. He himself came to believe that so much unearned wealth could be spiritually crippling, so he went to considerable lengths to dispense with the lot. This turned out to be a characteristically forthright manœuvre.

He went to the Realschule in Linz, along with Adolf Hitler, who was there at the same time. After that, came the Technische

Hochschule at Charlottenburg in Berlin, and then in 1908 he went to Manchester to study engineering. He came to preoccupy himself with the design of the propeller, thereby becoming entangled in the question of the foundations of mathematics. So thence to Frege, from him to Bertrand Russell in Cambridge, and from there to the Hardanger Fjord in Norway and the drafting of what would ultimately become the *Tractatus*. This would be finished at the end of the Great War.

Wittgenstein had volunteered to serve in the Austrian army, because he thought he had a duty to enlist as an Austrian citizen. Regarded by his family as the least brilliant of the boys, it had been thought that he should therefore be scheduled to perform some useful task in life. Three brothers committed suicide, and one, a pianist, had his arm blown off in combat, so played the piano with his left from that point on, commissioning works from distinguished composers such as Ravel in order to do so. And yet Russell told Wittgenstein's sister (to her utter astonishment) that this young man was the one expected to make the next significant step in philosophy.

After the war, and with the completion of the *Tractatus*, he disposed of his immense inheritance, which he did not want contaminating his mind, and went off to become a schoolteacher in Trattenbach in Lower Austria, having decided that he had already solved all philosophy's essential problems in his book. Things did not turn out well, however, since Wittgenstein was all his life enraged by anything he regarded as stupidity, even in schoolchildren, and he returned to Vienna, where he built a house for his sister Margarete. It is a monument to modernist rigour and exactitude, heavily indebted to the work and thought of Adolf Loos, whom he knew and admired, and who believed any form of ornamentation in architecture to be a crime. It can still be seen on Kundmangasse. The Wittgensteinhaus was subsequently to become the Bulgarian Cultural Institute. As long as communism lasted, the place was presumably a centre for melodramatic and largely bungled espionage. In 1929 Wittgenstein returned to Cambridge as a Fellow of Trinity College. By then he had already started to shift his attention from logic and the *Bild* theory, to 'grammar' as the expression of a 'form of life'.

TRACTATUS

AT THE TIME of the *Tractatus Logico-Philosophicus* Wittgenstein believed that the world (which is to say: 'everything that is the case') formulates itself in propositions. The logical form of any such proposition must share the structure of reality which it is expressing; it is isomorphic with the logical form inherent in the represented reality itself. At this point he believed that the grammar of logic was expressive, logically, of the structure of the reality it was articulating. So the formulation of the proposition constitutes an utterance of the structure of the reality being represented. Here the unthinkable is also the unsayable. If it cannot find lucid expression then it is not real thought at all, but mere nonsense. The picture (*Bild*) structured into the proposition permits a representation (*Darstellung*) of the underlying nature of things.

Wittgenstein believes that all the most significant truths in life can only be shown, not said; they say themselves in their own showing.

Some things however cannot be said; they can only be shown. That which can only be shown cannot 'say itself'. Wittgenstein gives a curious example of this, later in the *Philosophical Investigations*: If I know that the height of Mont Blanc is 15,771 feet, then it is meaningless to say that I know it, but cannot tell you. This is evidently the kind of knowledge where knowing and saying are inseparable; two sides of one coin. But what if I know the sound a clarinet makes? That is not something that can be 'said'. I can only take you to the clarinet while it is being played and show you. Many of the propositions towards the end of the *Tractatus* make it clear that Wittgenstein believes that all the most significant truths in life can only be shown, not said; they say themselves in their own showing. That which is sayable is a restricted sphere.

Wittgenstein read a great many philosophical works — with considerable intensity — but he had no interest whatsoever in 'the history of philosophy'. There was altogether too much academic baggage there, as far as he was concerned. Philosophy was happening now, with some urgency, or it was little more than some sort of university game, from which certain dubious characters made their living. Wittgenstein did not wish to be counted among their number, and often made his embarrassment all too clear whenever he was.

PHILOSOPHICAL INVESTIGATIONS.

A METAPHOR CAN lead you up a blind alley, as in this sentence. It can, like Morgan le Fay, so beguile and bewitch you with mists and imprecisions that your perceptions themselves become misted, your understanding flawed. Wittgenstein says this: 'Philosophy is a battle against the bewitchment of our intelligence by means of language.' Scepticism about the force of grammar, syntax and figures of speech is essential if the philosophical task is even to get properly started.

Whereas, in the *Tractatus*, logic and the picture theory of representation sought to remedy confusions, in the posthumously published *Philosophical Investigations* language is confronted with the tangle of its own sinuosities, the promptings that metaphor and usage provide us with, before 'thought' can even begin.

For Wittgenstein, philosophy is an activity, a method, and its function is to clarify the way we make valid statements…

All equations detect and calculate an equivalence in nature. So much energy can be derived from so much matter (given the necessary means required in order to release it). So much force applied in a particular direction will make a specified body accelerate thus. According to Wittgenstein, only natural science can actually *say* anything. Any knowledge to be had beyond this, as we have just seen, can only be shown. It is not the business of philosophy to 'derive truths' from its *material*; philosophy is an activity, a method, and its function is to clarify the way we make valid statements, the way we enact our propositions; the way we ensure that our representations have validity.

The source of our confusion is often this: we are implicated in the formulae of our meanings, without having analysed how language, syntax and figures of speech prompt us into the very thoughts they are structuring, and without providing any platform for viewing the mechanism of this same meaning-construction. The problem is that we cannot climb outside of language, since our only ladder and platform for such a procedure would be linguistic. Having climbed outside we simply discover that we are still inside after all, since the fire escape remains attached to the skin of the building.

After the isomorphic proposition and the *Bild* theory of representation of the *Tractatus*, Wittgenstein shifted his emphasis from logic to what he called grammar. It was grammar, he came to feel, which actually uttered those transcendental truths once referred to as metaphysics. Tomorrow never comes, so runs the old adage, and grammar confirms this fact. If tomorrow actually arrives then it must have translated itself into today. The only grammatical space where *tomorrow* might be activated is in the future perfect, and that is *ipso facto* a realm of illative speculation, since it is the nearest grammar ever comes to utopia.

In philosophy, we deal with description not explanation. Here Wittgenstein was heir to the tradition of Ernst Mach and Descriptionism, despite his insistence that reading Mach made him feel physically ill. He emphasized the importance of looking rather than assuming; the necessity to see before theorizing the sight. The question is this: how do we *mean*, and how do we *fail to mean*? All his life Wittgenstein was obsessed by the question of valid representation (or *Darstellung*), but the focus of that obsession shifted. He came to see how forms of life do not on the whole express themselves in logic's propositions, or logical notation, but instead in what he came to mean by his capacious notion of grammar.

Distrust of grammar, he claims, is the beginning of philosophy. Nietzsche too was aware of the perils of grammar, its unseen epistemological prompting; he seems to have reckoned that the noun commanding its verb in all our sentences leads us to suppose there must be a God, predicating his creation through the modal swerve of His grammatical omnipotence. And then there is the way grammar takes riotous control in the Alice books: "'I see nobody on the road," said Alice. "I only wish *I* had such eyes," the King remarked in a fretful tone. "To be able to see Nobody! And at that distance too! Why, it's as much as *I* can do to see real people, by this light!'" Nonsense this might be, but it is undoubtedly nonsense that has a logical method in it, and it also takes us back to Homer, where Odysseus informs the Cyclops that his name is *Outis*, which is to say '*no one*'. So when his neighbours come to ask what the cause of all the trouble is, and he replies *Outis*, they tell him to pipe down in that case and let them all get a little sleep. The literalizing of the metaphorical, the enfleshment of the linguistic abstraction, the foregrounding of the signifier over the signified – all these alert us to the potency of the figurative in shaping thought. And it is this same exercise that Wittgenstein engages in when he sets about puzzling through the meaning of Augustine's problems with the subject of time in the *Confessions*. He analyses how Augustine's bemusement regarding the nature of time arises out of the unexamined metaphor of time as a river; this brings with it all the implications, some of them seemingly contradictory, that proceed to befuddle his thought. He has not understood the directing force of his own controlling metaphor, so Wittgenstein sets about understanding it for him. And such clarification, such demystification, is the task of philosophy, whether in logic, in grammar, or in both.

ON CERTAINTY.

> Wittgenstein established for himself that all doubts entailed the employment of an intellectual machinery that needed to have some certainty embedded in it.

THE NOTION THAT a man in a cell knowing he is to be executed at dawn would decide that his only certainty in life is the fact that he is thinking, and knows himself to be thinking, might look, on examination, a trifle luxurious. Descartes lying abed until noon could well have arrived at such a conclusion, others however might not. For those others, in these circumstances, other certainties could seem equally pressing. Wittgenstein established for himself that all doubts entailed the employment of an intellectual machinery that needed to have some certainty embedded in it. Establishing a doubt with any confidence always involves the employment of some form of certainty, and to pretend otherwise amounts to a form of philosophical dishonesty.

In the 1930s the writer Robert Walser was in a sanatorium in Switzerland. People would sometimes come to see him. One such visitor asked him about his writing. 'I am not here to write,' he said. 'I am here to be mad.' That statement surely indicates a remarkable clarity of mind in one diagnosed as a paranoid schizophrenic – the term was apparently invented to describe his condition. At the same moment the Ballets Russes star Nijinsky was also housed in an asylum, and he would patiently explain that he had once been a notable dancer, but now he was a horse. That misconception isn't 'a mistake', in Wittgenstein's formulation, so much as an ontological confusion. Certainty here constitutes a kind of blindness to your actual condition, though it is a curiosity that if I had asked about the condition in later life of Nijinsky in the 1980s, the likelihood is that my interlocutor would have started talking about a horse; that would have been the Canadian thoroughbred who'd had the dancer's name bestowed upon him. A proper name is usually thought to be the final capstan on epistemology's quay, a guarantor of identity. There we are meant to encounter an irrefutable *quidditas*. Yet here we have (1) Nijinsky the man and (2) Nijinsky the horse. And for a while (1) was convinced he was (2). What certainty is to be had in names and identity here, we might ask? Whose certainty is to be certified?

We might remember too that when Gulliver returns from the land of the Houyhnhnms he is so ashamed of being a Yahoo (albeit a gentle one) that he loathes the company of his wife and child in the house, and prefers whenever possible to spend his time in the stable, where the smell of horses (and the groom) reminds him of the Houyhnhnms. He though cannot, like Nijinsky, tell himself he is a horse. He only wishes he could. Gulliver suffers not from any ontological confusion but from an alienating confusion of the affections. He has lived for so long in the oxygen tent of lofty Houyhnmhnm reasoning and now he must return to the contaminated air of eighteenth-century England. It is possible he has confused himself by an over-indulgence in unhelpful rationalist certainties. The unrelenting reasoning of the Houyhnhnms has made him forget what Keats called 'the holiness of the heart's affections'. He has become intellectually and emotionally displaced from his own species. This can be read as a satire on Enlightenment presumption, or it can be viewed as an epiphenomenon of Swift's loathing for so many of his own wretched kind.

Either way, certainty is not simply a matter of making mistakes. Wittgenstein was very clear about this and he detested the way J. G. Frazer in *The Golden Bough* treated mythology as though it were an early, bungled attempt at science; primitive culture getting previous with itself before it had the necessary intellectual equipment to formulate an array of appropriate equations. His annotations on *The Golden Bough* show his rising irritation. This is too big to be a mistake, he says. What we are observing is a form of life, one which includes magic. And what magic presents us with is a wish injected into a representation.

THE VIENNESE CONTEXT.

MANY OF THE ENTRIES in this splendid two-volume compendium published by Bloomsbury relate to Vienna. The opening chapter is from Toulmin and Janik's superb *Wittgenstein's Vienna*, and it describes the city in its pre-war days, the place Karl Kraus once called a laboratory for world destruction. This was the city of Klimt and Schiele, of Mach and Bolzmann, of Adolf Loos, whose article 'Ornamentation and Crime' appeared in 1908 in the *Frankfurter Zeitung*. In the city of the Ringstrasse this Viennese architect announced that ornamentation was crime; that style in architecture must be indistinguishable from function. 'Functionalism', as an architectural doctrine, dates back to Loos, and when Wittgenstein turned his mind to architecture, he employed Loos's principles in doing so. What Wittgenstein did, in building the house for his sister, was precisely what he had done in the *Tractatus*: strip the particular activity of everything inessential, try to express the fundaments of the activity by unrelenting logic. Wittgenstein's original wish had been to study with Bolzmann in Vienna, but the latter had committed suicide in 1906.

STYLE.

> **Wittgenstein insists that style is a spiritual achievement, that the pellucidity of expression we call style can be distinguished from mere fashion only by the full engagement of the spirit.**

Wittgenstein came from the Vienna of Adolf Loos and Karl Kraus. The architect and the satirist both had something in common: the conviction that style was the expression of morality, not a mere confection that might be assembled above it. Style was the ultimate expression of identity. A confused or deceitful style meant a confused or deceitful person. Wittgenstein indicates several times in *Culture and Value* that good style is integral to good philosophising; he appears to be announcing how style, when well-fashioned, facilitates and exhibits thought. But he says more than that: he insists that style is a spiritual achievement, that the pellucidity of expression we call style can be distinguished from mere fashion only by the full engagement of the spirit. In writing, style is the economic alignment of linguistic resource and authorial intention. It is technical virtuosity allied to acceleration of spirit. The stylist in written form needs to be alert to language — its resonance, density and promise. And style (in its variegated protocols and requirements) precedes the author. It is then a two-way transaction, between the language and the individual, the individual and the intellectual matrix in which he is situated; it is a Janus-faced accomplishment, a negotiation between tradition and the individual talent.

To become an accomplished stylist is most certainly not to behave unilaterally towards your linguistic environment; that might mark you out as a Dadaist, a Tristan Tzara, assaulting the language in protest at its lethal instrumentalism in coordinating the Great War. It is instead to take the full force of the historical language as it presents itself synchronically and diachronically, and learn to find your individual way inside and through it. Every stylist, whatever else he is, must be a minotaur in the linguistic labyrinth into which he has been inserted; that *Dasein* of which Heidegger speaks.

Style is not an egotistical imposition on language, but rather its lucid and efficient habitation. It is a way of grasping how language and usage, the dictionary and the street hawker, express between them a 'form of life' that must be mentally inhabited if it is to be linguistically exploited. The achievement of style is the lucid and effective insertion of one's individual ability into the world of linguistic possibility.

Wittgenstein's own style always tended towards the atomistic and fragmented; he was sceptical regarding the techniques employed to solder together large discursive wholes. His forebears here include Lichtenberg, Spinoza and Nietzsche.

THE LINGUISTIC TURN.

WE CAN COME TO see certain historic shifts in our thought with subsequent clarity. We now understand how the antiquarian view gave way to the archaeological one, or how creation stopped being dated scripturally and was instead re-inscribed according to Lyell's principles of geology and stratigraphy. We observe how the story of humankind ceased to be post-Adamic and post-Edenic, and translated itself instead into a study that was palæontological and fossil-based. This required a much greater antiquity for our human origins. We finally abandoned the notion of special creation and accepted Darwin's mutation and evolution of species, in the mighty and variegated struggle for survival. 'There is special providence in the fall of a sparrow,' says Hamlet. Maybe so, but that providential eye appears to have blinked pretty massively during the great extinctions. Were Wittgenstein's work ever to be universally accepted, it might effect an equivalent shift in modes of thought to some of those mentioned above. We would understand how our forms of life always generate metaphoric systematicities, inside which we live. The language shapes itself around and through our world of activity and reflection. Language and its morphologies are always both social and teleological. There can be no private language: language always enacts and expresses our interaction with nature and with one another. And the notion of a philosopher as someone with a specialised paraphernalia of thought who can thereby arrive at elevated metaphysical termini closed off to the rest of us, is simply risible.

> **The notion of a philosopher as someone with a specialised paraphernalia of thought...is simply risible.**

One way to discuss this is to see Wittgenstein as a philosophical expression of that shift in awareness and analysis commonly known as 'the linguistic turn'. But here we must tread with care. The *Tractatus* was in effect an attempt to escape (or at least bypass) the linguistic turn; to find a mode of expression not entangled in the densities of language, but capable of uttering an essential structure of reality detachable from the workings of any specific language. It is in the work subsequent to the *Tractatus* that Wittgenstein explores the significance of the linguistic turn from the inside, exploring the way language structures our thought, and expresses our form of life.

IN THE WEB OF LANGUAGE.

DAVID BOHM ARGUED that the reality of elementary particles might be better conveyed by verbs than by nouns; that their nature was more verbal than nominal. It would make more sense to say 'to electron' than to talk about 'an electron'. 'The meaning of a word,' Wittgenstein tells us, 'is its use in the language.' In the Preface to his great *Dictionary* of 1755, Samuel Johnson came (ruefully) to the same conclusion. Usage ultimately dictates meaning, however much the lexicographer might shake his head, bewigged or not. It is no use etymologising, for if a word has shifted its ground, then the ground on which it stands is thereby redefined. The word *sely* in

Chaucer means pure and blameless; it subsequently becomes *silly*. The word *internecine* originally meant mutually harmful; it now means mutually destructive, by an apparent fluke. Usage always takes command.

In the structuralist linguistics of De Saussure, the diachronic axis tells us how the morphemic units arrived and acquired their current morphology and significance. But it is the synchronic system at any moment that will show us how each word actually functions. Dandelion, daisy, primrose, cowslip – all these words have fascinating etymologies: teeth of the lion, the day's eye, the first rose, and cow slime. But as long as I can point to the individual plants and use these words competently in my ostensive display, then I am linguistically competent. The etymologies (those diachronic dimensions) are not required for competent linguistic performance in the synchronic moment of utterance.

Various essays in these two volumes remind us how much of his early life Wittgenstein spent looking at and using engineering diagrams.

There is often something diagrammatic about Wittgenstein's thought (as John Berger has pointed out, there is also something diagrammatic about Cubism). Various essays in these two volumes remind us how much of his early life Wittgenstein spent looking at and using engineering diagrams. At the origins of language and writing we find pictography, and pictography finds its modern descendent in the diagram. The diagram achieved one of its most splendid modern incarnations in the 1931 London Underground

Map of Harry Beck, still in use today. We see there what diagrams are for: to analyse a system into its inter-related functions, and then proceed to portray those functions with ruthless simplification. That in one sense is what Wittgenstein was attempting with the atomic propositions in the *Tractatus*.

But grammar contains its own logic, however arbitrary some of its rules might be. Even the grammatical rule that distinguishes between mass (or quantity) nouns and counting nouns also enunciates a truth: I cannot give you a sugar, because it is a quantity not a particle. I can give you a grain of sugar, because grains can be counted out one by one. I cannot give you a little human, but I can give you a little human being. Grammar will usually be found to be functioning according to its own discernible logic, but it is not self-foundational (any more, Wittgenstein believed, than philosophy could ever be), and it can often be seen to operate arbitrarily. Why is it that if I talk of more than one newspaper empire I must say media, but if I meet more than one spiritual channeller at a séance, I must speak of mediums? Either way, we are witnessing the expression of what Wittgenstein called a form of life. Grammar in this wide sense is a crucial enunciation of the form of life the speakers inhabit.

The notion that experience, in travelling through the sensorium of one who happens to be a philosopher, translates itself into wisdom, where the common man can only expect at best common sense – this notion was repellent to Wittgenstein. He also found absurd the thought that arriving at philosophical truth could be viewed as a form of specialism – like an optometrist arriving at conclusions about eyes. And his lifelong target became that ghost of rationality testing out its presuppositions in the Cartesian mental schema.

> **Philosophic thought for Wittgenstein is…a technique for clarifying the confusions which language is easily able to bring about through its own operations. Clarify the language and the problem disappears.**

Philosophic thought for Wittgenstein is not an assembly of perceptions and opinions. Nor is it an array of reflective 'conclusions'. It is instead a technique for clarifying the confusions which language is easily able to bring about through its own operations. The problem will be solved when it is realised that it was created in the first place by a confusion of thought inhabiting a confusion of language. Clarify the language, unmangle the mangled thought, and the problem promptly disappears. It is in this sense that he came increasingly to believe that all genuine philosophy is a form of *Sprachkritik*, or a critique of language and its usage.

THE WORLD OF FACTUALITY.

LYING BEHIND WITTGENSTEIN'S notion of the fact, however mystical some of his early expressions might appear, is that world of factuality established by post-Galilean experimental science. In the face of traditional authority, however elevated, Galileo (like Francis Bacon) says, *prove it*. Aristotle claimed that a heavier body falls to earth faster than a lighter one. All right then, here are two planks. Let's send a heavier ball down one and a lighter down the other.

Conclusion? Aristotle was wrong. *Nullius in verba* was the motto of the Royal Society. Don't take anyone's word for it. Just because that has been the tradition does not make it true. Now, the world of science borders on the world of mythology. It is astonishing sometimes how superstitions prevail even at the edges of science. It took a long time before everyone agreed that swallows do not hibernate at the bottom of ponds during the winter. Or that smeared garlic will not disable any magnet; that its needle will not cease to quiver towards true north in its presence. Joseph Priestley was one of the most impressive scientists of his day, but he would not relinquish the notion of phlogiston, an essence of fieriness that never in fact existed. He also believed at the time of the French Revolution that Jesus would return to establish his Kingdom on earth within thirty years. Which of the two beliefs appears the more unreasonable might now be a moot point.

The word *fact* starts to detach itself from an action (frequently a criminal one) sometime in the mid-seventeenth century. In the world of natural science, at least, it starts to become instead an establishable reality, a provable datum of the observable world. Experiment can now establish the distinction between superstition and fact. Test it; try it out; sort out the fiction from the fact. *Nullius in verba*

The old usage continues, in tributaries here and there. We have this in Jane Austen's *Emma*: 'Gracious in fact if not in word.' And here in the Prologue to Wilkie Collins' *The Moonstone*: ' …that any thief detected in the fact, be he whom he might, should be hung.' And we have the legalistic survival 'accessory after the fact'. But the world of fact in the philosophy of positivism or scientism soon starts to bulldoze its way towards a new metaphysic and a comprehensive epistemology. It then took A. N. Whitehead in the sciences, and Georges Braque in the arts, to insist that there is no such thing (and never had been any such thing) as a solitary fact. To think in a way that imagines there ever could be constitutes a grave distortion of the way we must construct any world of meaning. A fact only gains its factuality by virtue of its situation in a domain of agreed perception and proof. Or as Braque put it in his *Notebooks*: 'There are no things; only relations between things.' The artistic proof of this statement is Cubism. Facts confirm 'forms of life', by exhibiting their structures, in the same way that Harry Beck's Underground Map tells us a great deal about the nature of communication in the English metropolis.

THE SHIFT IN EMPHASIS.

THE WORLD OF pure logic subsists on tautologies. It is in one sense a world of perfectly symmetrical vacuity, a world which the *Tractatus* sought to enunciate. Once synthetic *a priori* statements enter the field, information has started arriving from the natural world. With synthetic *a posteriori* statements we start to be bombarded with so many multifarious phenomena that we need what the Descriptionists called an economy of thought in order to sort through them. In their view, this cognitive economy was called science. We economise thought into propositions deserving assent in order to resist our own intellectual inundation by the phenomenal whirligig. We work out and encode what sayings have meaning, and are verifiable, so as to situate ourselves with exactitude inside the world of nature. The great difference between Wittgenstein and those who thought they were his followers (like the members of the *Wiener Kreis*) is that they thought science could say everything worth saying, with logic's assistance. Wittgenstein thought the most important things still remained unsaid. And could never be said, though some could (for a time, anyway) be shown. Later in life he abandoned the distinction between saying and showing; he came to inhabit language entirely, the way an archaeologist inhabits ruins, searching for the logic in the fragments.

LANGUAGE AND THE ENGINEERING OF OUR THOUGHT.

THE FIRST SENTENCE of the *Blue Book* is 'What is the meaning of a word?' The answer comes a few pages later: the life of a sign is its use. Or as Wittgenstein says elsewhere, the meaning of a word is its use in the language. There can be no meaning separate from the system of signs in which the word is employed; in this he appears to be entirely in agreement with the work of De Saussure, to whom he never alludes, and whose work he probably never encountered.

There is no occult realm of correspondences in which the sign has meaning bestowed upon it by a mental potency. We constantly talk as though there is, but this is, Wittgenstein reckons, a mistake. It is the system of signs itself that assigns meaning; it is only in the system of signs that a word acquires and maintains (or changes) its use, which is to say its meaning. Is there no meaning then, which does not travel through this conduit of language? Some can think musically or mathematically, but even these apparently non-linguistic systems of representation must still express some aspect of Wittgenstein's *Lebensform* or 'form of life'. They can never be entirely unrelated to language, for *homo sapiens sapiens* at this late stage in the game can never become non-linguistic.

Wittgenstein's early training, as we have seen, was in engineering, and he had become accustomed to staring hard at technical drawings. He is much less discursive than most other philosophers. He is looking for the atomistic elements that make up the general picture before us, and his thinking is frequently focused, though not necessarily spatial. But it strives to be diagrammatic. What is it that a diagram does? It accepts the formality of its representational identity, and never pretends that it can escape it, so it simplifies and visualizes functions into ideogrammatic images. It formulates propositions which seek to be isomorphic with that situation which they represent.

All Wittgenstein's hermeneutic activities pointed him towards the nomothetic, which is to say, the detection and articulation of laws. He wants to know how we can know; by what cognitive procedures and heuristic protocols we come by our knowledge. He concludes that it is not by the construction of an inner language; nor is it by contemplation of a bodiless and ethereal *I*. That mythic *I* which is the foundational principle of Cartesian philosophy is one of his most recurrent targets, for that *I* labours under the illusion that it might ultimately be separable from language.

William James in *Principles of Psychology* points out that the peril of any supposed process of apperception might be to imagine that if one turns up the gas speedily enough, one might get a better glimpse of the darkness. When we bring observation to bear upon the subatomic world, we change that which we would observe by the very act of looking, by our energetic appraisal itself, and when we think we are gazing into the self, it is inevitably the self that is doing the gazing, even as it objectifies that gaze into a self the self might have gazed into. Here we do indeed inhabit the hall of mirrors of thought. We might need an engineer to point out to us how it came to be constructed.

WHAT ARE WE GIVEN?

THE ONLY *A PRIORI* in Wittgenstein's philosophy by the end is this: the existence of the *Lebensformen*. Inside these we live, and through these we express ourselves. Descartes' notion of the spectral reason locked up in the individual identity is a misrepresentation of who and how we are. One of Francis Bacon's popes shrieking silently inside the ghostly gridiron of his *baldachino*: that might well be the Cartesian ego translated back to its ontological solitude. Distrust it, says Wittgenstein, for it is a philosophical fantasy. We might say: one day one solipsist's territory was invaded by another solipsist. But it ended well, since neither of them noticed.

Wittgenstein's fascination with religious forms baffled many of the positivists who imagined he was their ally.

Wittgenstein's fascination with religious forms baffled many of the positivists who imagined he was their ally. For such ceremonious creatures as ourselves, he seems to say, blessed with speech and custom as we are, a sacrifice might well be necessitated, as the only means of centering our lives, not to mention our deaths. We must not, however, think of ourselves as being defective angels with most of our more divine faculties tuned out. The Fall might make us all apprentices in sensibility and intellection, but it is an ongoing Fall, not an ontological priority.

No one has ever put more definitive quotation marks around the notion 'I' than Wittgenstein: they are both emboldened and italicized. One feels that – had typographic convention permitted – they would have been capitalized too. Basil Fawlty, attempting to grasp a German guest's complaint, asks him to speak more slowly. '*Ich*', begins the guest. 'We'll come back to that,' says Basil. And that seems to have been pretty much Wittgenstein's line too. We keep coming back to that *I*: what precisely is it? Can we ever really fit inside such a condensed locution, such an elliptical glyph?

BEGINNINGS.

WITTGENSTEIN DOES NOT APPEAR to have spent much time brooding on the actual origins of language. The notion that there was a single language that was the *fons et origo* of our linguistic history is known as monogenesis. This would have had to have been that *Lingua adamica* of which Böhme spoke. The favoured language in this originary myth has often been Hebrew, since — if we believe the inherited texts — that was the tongue spoken by Adam and Eve in Eden, in the linguistic moment of genesis, the language that must be closest to creation. The alternative to this theory was polygenesis: languages occurred all over the place, developing side by side; they *developed*. Languages emerged as the expression of, and the negotiation with, our multifarious forms of life. They are utterances, in linguistic form, of *Lebensformen*. They are part of our vast collective self-engineering.

One year after the publication of the *Tractatus* in 1922, Le Corbusier published *Vers Une Architecture*. The similarities are startling. Le Corbusier contrasts the architect, obsessing over his historical styles, with the engineer: the latter has to find an economy of form and function. That is why Le Corbusier is more impressed with the design of ocean liners, grain elevators, motor cars and aeroplanes than he is with so many modern buildings: engineers are engineering answers right now to current problems; these solutions do not wear fancy dress, as historicist architecture (like that on the *Ringstrasse*) so often does. Here Le Corbusier is looking at the making of buildings the way an engineer looks at the problems of speed or storage, and in the *Tractatus*, Wittgenstein was looking at the problems of philosophy the way an engineer looks at the problem of locomotion. Both of them wanted to get back to the fundamentals of their trade.

Later on, for Wittgenstein, grammar comes to mean the way in which we use language, and sometimes the way in which language uses us. Unexamined metaphors control our thought through a grammatical insistence we have grown all-too-casually accustomed to. His distinction between deep and surface grammar (*Tiefengrammatik* and *Oberflächengrammatik*) suggests that grammar in its full sense is the spectral sublime of language, the skeleton key of semiology. Grammar expresses the essence of meaning, as Wittgenstein put it.

A UNITY AMONGST THE DISTINCTIONS.

WITTGENSTEIN DID TO philosophy what the Great War did to the Austro-Hungarian Empire: he shook it to its foundations, refusing to recognise any previous boundaries or frontiers. So for that matter, the Wittgensteinhaus is to the historicist style of the Viennese *Ringstrasse* what Wittgenstein's philosophy was to so much that had immediately preceded it: a demolition of all unwanted ornamentation, a return to fundamentals, the same strategy in thought as an Adolf Loos building in architecture.

> **Wittgenstein did to philosophy what the Great War did to the Austro-Hungarian Empire: he shook it to its foundations…**

As we already noted, in one sense the *Tractatus* is a desperate attempt to avoid the implications of the linguistic turn, in the density of its linguistic complications, and *Philosophical Investigations* is in contrast an acceptance of its consequences, still the same obsession remains: the attempt to find the form of valid representations. What can we actually say that isn't flummery, and what mode do we need to employ in which to say it?

Some of Wittgenstein's remarks never leave you. His observation that if a lion could speak, we would not understand a word he said is one. So different is the lion's form of life that even were we to share a lexis and a syntax, we would share nothing it would be possible to say to one another. There would be nothing intelligible between us. He also insisted that the best image of the human soul was the human face. One can imagine how the sadness in the expression of the last Neanderthal was a form of critique of the voracious new predator (a different version of *homo sapiens* from himself, that was for sure) with whom he had been cohabiting on the Iberian peninsula, though not for much longer. How much time this new fellow spent mouthing those curious noises of his. Sometimes alone, all to himself. And how superbly he had started making those new weapons.

WITTGENSTEIN'S BELIEFS.

THERE HAS BEEN much speculation about Wittgenstein's beliefs, and in particular if they really took a religious form. We know that he abandoned any species of institutional belief in his early teens, and never subsequently expressed a wish to re-join a confessional community. We also know that he had the greatest respect for religion, in all its forms, and that he was preoccupied for the whole of his life with Christianity. At the end of the war, he always carried about his copy of Tolstoy's *Gospel in Brief*, so much so that he was known to his fellow soldiers as either the Gospel Man or the Tolstoy Man. What Tolstoy had done in this book was to use his writer's intelligence to work out what he believed to be the aspects of Jesus's life that could be accepted by an intelligent believer. He cut out the miracles and the resurrection, and there was no mention of that divine origin which so preoccupies John at the beginning of his gospel. What we are presented with instead is probably the same Jesus that Matthew Arnold believed to be there at the beginning of the Christian tradition, before all the supernatural additions were provided, in order, he reckoned, to provide gewgaws and baubles for the credulous. Reasons to believe that were entirely contrary to reason.

He believed that a fable in art, like a proposition in philosophy, could shape a valid truth into memorable expression.

We also know that Wittgenstein greatly admired the late tales of Tolstoy, and for the same reason that he admired early Westerns:

they both provided in compressed and lucid form fables by which we might try to understand our condition. He believed that a fable in art, like a proposition in philosophy, could shape a valid truth into memorable expression. He believed that philosophy, and any person with any philosophical integrity, should put its money where its mouth is, and not go about pretending to know what it does not (and cannot) in truth know. And so he was profoundly allergic to that breezy polysyllabic blather that sometimes passes for thought in the academy.

Wittgenstein as a Universal Antonym for 'Yes-man'.

ALTHOUGH MANY OF the pieces published in these two impressive volumes would be known already to Wittgensteinians, many more would not. Unless you have not only bought anthologies like Rush Rees's *Recollections of Wittgenstein*, but also followed such publications as *Guy's Hospital Reports* and the *Irish Medical Times*, or *Hermathena*, then some of these essays will be new to you. Together they present a composite image of the man which is hugely impressive. Perhaps each century can produce one man like Wittgenstein; certainly not many more. What impresses most about him is the utter integrity with which he approached every day in his life, every page he wrote, every relationship in which he seriously engaged. If there is a universal antonym for 'jobsworth' and 'yes-man', it could well be Wittgenstein. From his insistence on serving in the Austrian army (medically, he would have been exempt) and getting himself to the front, to his insistence on giving up his vast fortune, we see a man who takes what life offers seriously, who does not simply slide by. I find myself remembering Geoffrey Hill's magnificent lines in his tribute to Charles Péguy:

Must men stand by what they write
as by their camp-beds or their weaponry
or shell-shocked comrades while they sag and cry?

Wittgenstein stood by what he wrote, and was rightly contemptuous of those who did not. Yet how they seem to thrive…

10.

Irony and Ironists

IRONY: IS IT FATAL?

'IF THIS IS DYING, then I don't think much of it.' So said Lytton Strachey on his deathbed, with grave irony. The irony consists in the fact that it did not matter in the slightest what he thought of it; nor could he take it or leave it, death being no respecter of human choice. Many years before, Strachey had been equally ironic, once again concerning a matter of life and death. Appearing before a military tribunal which was assessing his claim to be treated as a conscientious objector, he was asked by the chairman what he would do should he see a German soldier attempting to violate his sister. 'I should try to interpose my body,' he is said to have replied. The irony of this was not lost on his gay friends, although the outcome might well have been much the same as on the later occasion, since not all German soldiers shared the proclivities of those whom Christopher Isherwood met in the dark streets of the Weimar Republic. Henry James, perceiving the approach of the finale, said: 'So here it is at last, the distinguished thing.' The thing might be distinguished but it is also generic and unclassifiable, even for this expert word-user, since as Wittgenstein remarked, death is not an event in life.

An ironist is one who detects how loosely we inhabit those meanings and values which (we keep insisting) fit us as tightly as our skin.

So can one go ironically to one's death? Did even Socrates, that great ironist, manage it? As the hemlock chilled its way through his body, did he retain his sense of play between overt statement and hidden truth? An ironist is one who detects how loosely we inhabit those meanings and values which (we keep insisting) fit us as tightly as our skin. No, says the ironist, you cannot change your skin, unless you are Michael Jackson — and see how well that gambit turned out in the end — but you can certainly change your meanings and values, depending on your desires, and your variable chances of survival at any particular moment. The ironist lets us know how breezy all our confidence in singular meaning might yet turn out to be:

> Oh, life is a glorious cycle of song,
> A medley of extemporanea;
> And love is a thing that can never go wrong;
> And I am Marie of Romania.

Thus the ever-ironic Dorothy Parker, and her example is a good one. What the ironist says is a matter of logic: if this, then that. But since *that* is not inevitably that, then *this* is not inevitably this either. Forgive me pointing it out, my unironised friend, but you are living in cloud-cuckoo land. Which is hardly a solid basis for anyone's epistemology. And when you find yourself unfriended in heaven, by the interloper's upwardly mobile cuckoo chicks, you might have to fall a long way on your journey back to earth.

The crucifix is a visual emblem of contradiction. How the vertical is crossed by the horizontal. How the body of a man, hoisted high for everyone to see, soon loses its ability to continue. And the *Logia of Jeshua* seem to be recording a prophet who delighted in turning every old truth inside out. Love your friends? Too easy: love your enemies as well. Someone gives you a belt in the face? Good: now turn the unbruised side of your face around, and let him have a whack at that too. These, in the widest sense, are ironic manoeuvres. But it is possible that the ultimate irony – one that travelled far beyond him, were the words he cried out according to the Gospel of Mark and Matthew: '*Eli, Eli, lama sabachthani?*' Which is to say, 'My God, my God, why have you deserted me?' That power, whom Jesus called Abba, or Father, and which had appeared to be an endless source of identity and strength within him, now appeared gone, when he needed it most. If this is an irony, then it is the bitterest one of all. Irony might appear too urbane a word, in a situation of such savage extremity. Or perhaps not. One of Jesus's most characteristic ironic manoeuvres was to draw attention to the materiality of that which can appear entirely transparent and vehicular: the Law, for example. If you wish to stone to death one you have found morally compromised, perhaps you might examine your own fitness to be the agency of such Law. Or take a look at the coins with which you pay the tribute money. Whose image is embossed upon it? That of Caesar? Then you have already accepted how such coins gain their authority from him, so why not offer them back? This foregrounding of the materiality of the sign is a constant of the ironic mode, often in its most comedic incarnations. When Vincent begs Mia in Tarantino's *Pulp Fiction*: 'If you're alive, say something,' she replies, 'Something'.

COSMIC IRONY.

WE CERTAINLY TALK as though an irony can be created without any particular ironist sitting down to construct it. The ultimate cosmic irony might be this: in the geological era some now call the Anthropocene, since humanity has finally started changing the climate and the structure of the earth itself, Anthropos could find himself annihilated, almost as soon as he has inaugurated a geological era containing his own nomenclature. What goes around comes around. The dinosaurs had no name for themselves until seventy million years after their own extinction, and they were never the ones to utter it.

Irony, whether written or natural, is a dialectic between meaning and non-meaning; between presence and absence. Irony demonstrates that all meanings can disappear into themselves as well as manifesting themselves before us. Meaning in the ironic schema is binary: now you see it now you don't. Like the object in the magician's black glove it only shows itself so it can disappear again. Irony is a form of semantic bilocation. And the ironist's ultimate destination, as that great ironist Beckett understood, could well be silence. Only thus might one escape what Kierkegaard understood to be the weighty and unrelenting burden of the ironist everywhere: subjective negativity. (It was also Kierkegaard's perception that when the ironic gaze suffers the irruption of humour, then we find ourselves looking not merely at the paradoxes of finitude, but at the paradox of sin too.)

Irony in its verbal form is a distance between this meaning and that one; sometimes the two meanings attach to the one word. So when Mark Antony keeps uttering the word 'honourable', in regard to Brutus and the other republican assassins, with each reiteration the word peels itself all the more resolutely away from those men to whom it claims to be attached. Repetition here can be seen to iterate a separation.

At times the irony can be contained inside the single word itself, with no further reference to the lexical beyond. Nabokov gives us this little definition of *eros*: the rose and the sore. Here the word anagrammatizes itself into two hemispheres, one of joy and one of misery. The perception, one suspects, might have been an insomniac one, and Nabokov was a legendary insomniac. The same effect recurs throughout Shakespeare's Sonnets, though we know nothing regarding that man's sleeping habits, even if Macbeth's sleeplessness is the most terrifying evocation of insomnia in the language.

In cosmic irony the structure happens to be the structure of everything…And the Freudian irony runs along a parallel line: civilization makes us neurotically ill.

In rhetoric it is traditional to distinguish between verbal and structural irony. In the latter some specific event or characterisation is contrasted to the irony of the whole narrative itself, the way the story contradicts itself, or annihilates its own apparent progress by a certain turn of events. In cosmic irony the structure happens to be the structure of everything. So the Darwinian irony is this: only through our expertise in various techniques of savagery, hunting and slaughter, did we manage to create civilization. And the Freudian irony runs along a parallel line: civilization makes us neurotically ill. For each one of us individually, it often seems to be too great a price to pay. But there is no credit relief to be had in the world of the socialised psyche. Like the fly and its legendary amber, we're stuck with it and in it.

In *Macbeth*, the structural irony is the fact that the promises of the Weird Sisters turn out to be lethal equivocations. As the subsequent progress of Macbeth shows, it is not a good idea to base your career (not to mention your eschatology) on a quibble. It is possible that the greatest structural irony in *Hamlet* is that Claudius is Hamlet's natural father. The King was, after all, away a great deal, and Gertrude does seem remarkably pleased to be receiving the attentions of her brother-in-law of some decades. She'd had a long enough time to work out whether or not she liked him. So it could be that the Prince, in seeking to avenge his supposed father's murder, actually brings about his biological father's death, not to mention his mother's, Ophelia's, Polonius's, and his own. In *The Godfather*, the ultimate moment of structural irony comes at the beginning when Michael announces 'That's my family, Kay, it's not me.' The rest of the film proves that Michael *is* his family. All its Sicilian values of vendetta and vengeance are decanted into him.

STYLE.

THE IRONIST'S LIFELINE through the story (textual and biographical) is style. And *style* here means precision. Lexis, syntax and punctuation must all be as sharp as a scalpel if the surgical incisions are to be made effective. In Beckett's *Krapp's Last Tape*, the eponymous hero contemplates his hoped-for literary success of many years thus: 'Seventeen copies sold, of which eleven at trade price to free circulating libraries beyond the seas. Getting known.' One only has to substitute 'nearly twenty' for 'seventeen' to see how the precision here works to such effect. Mathematics applied to the human organism and its doings becomes one of Beckett's hallmarks, as here in *Molloy*:

> And in winter, under my greatcoat, I wrapped myself in swathes of newspaper, and did not shed them until the earth awoke, for good, in April. The *Times Literary Supplement* was admirably adapted to this purpose, of a never-failing toughness and impermeability. Even farts made no impression on it. I can't help it, gas escapes from my fundament on the least pretext, it's hard not to mention it now and then, however great my distaste. One day I counted them. Three hundred and fifteen farts in nineteen hours, or an average of over sixteen farts an hour. After all, it's not excessive. Four farts every fifteen minutes. It's nothing.
>
> Not even one fart every four minutes. It's unbelievable. Damn it, I hardly fart at all, I should never have mentioned it.

Such precisions make the human predicament comical, and seem to confirm Bergson's view that humour frequently occurs when the human appears before us with machine-like motions. Charlie Chaplin in *Modern Times* achieves this effect supremely when he is swallowed by the machine he is meant to be tending.

And then there is the magisterial and collusive overview, where the author appears to be conniving with the mendacity and greed of those whose history he is currently recounting. Here is Evelyn Waugh in *Scoop*, recounting the success of the Jackson family in Ishmaelia, after the success of its first President, Mr Samuel Smiles Jackson:

> …a choice whose wisdom seemed to be confirmed by history, for, forty years later, a Mr Rathbone Jackson held his grandfather's office in succession to his father Pankhurst, while the chief posts of the state were held by Messrs Garnett Jackson, Mander Jackson, Huxley Jackson, his uncle and brothers, and by Mrs Athol (*née* Jackson) his aunt. So strong was the love which the Republic bore the family that General Elections were known as "Jackson Ngomas" wherever and whenever they were held.

The author and his style have here become collusive with the corrupt practices which they portray. As the details pile up, the cohesive surface fractures in a formal overload to produce that dissonant effect which is always the endpoint of irony, for irony is the kingdom of dissonance, a dissonance achieved by precision of detail and phrasing, apparently at variance with the overview being propounded. The style holds the content in place just long enough, until the effective content finds itself reversed. Then the first are seen to be last and the last first. We are in that topsy-turvy land where the ironist reckons most of us live anyway.

In *Black Mischief,* Waugh satirised an independent African country, Azania. He is often criticised for the implied racism of this novel. What the critics frequently miss is that, if Waugh satirises the Africans, he satirises the Europeans and Americans at least as much. The central source of mischief in the book is the upper-class Englishman, Basil Seal. A Seal, when it emerges from its element, is black. It is Basil, after all, who consumes his casual lover Prudence, in a cannibal feast which appears to be a horrific parody of the Eucharistic meal. The editor of a Catholic weekly, *The Tablet*, was so appalled by the book that he used his own pages to question publicly whether the new convert really deserved to be a member of the Roman Catholic Church at all.

REVERSAL AS REVELATION.

Turn your wisdom on its head, reverse what you imagine to be your immemorial *doxa***, and see what revelations might then follow.**

IF, AS HAS often been speculated, the man we call Jesus was known before his death by means of the circulation of the *Logia of Yeshua*, then his primary trope, the one that drew so much attention to him, would appear to be reversal. If that prophet and healer had one thing in common with Oscar Wilde (apart from the fact of persecution) it was this. Take any well-known saying, particularly one of those in the moral sphere, and turn it on its head. We have, it would appear, so utterly misconstrued the Lord's intentions as to proceed widdershins, rather than the right way about. Turn your wisdom on its head, reverse what you imagine to be your immemorial *doxa*, and see what revelations might then follow. You think the poor are the wretched of the earth, but they're the ones who have first place in the Kingdom of Heaven. You think your possessions are a sign of God's approval, but if you truly want to do His will, you must give them all away. The possessions you took to be rewards for your virtue are signposts to hell.

Wilde's formulations were often of a similar nature. Take a well-known phrase or saying – for example, 'Drink is the curse of the working classes' – and reverse it: 'Work is the curse of the drinking classes.' It has a momentary shock effect, a frisson, though if the device is repeated often enough it can become both mechanical and tiresome. As one wag once parodied the procedure: 'Well, it may not be salt, but it certainly is pepper.' But in Wilde's most important works, like the essay 'The Soul of Man Under Socialism', the technique is both morally daring, and revelatory. Soon enough it was to lead to his undoing.

The technique of taking the least expected route into a subject became such a reflex that Wilde could not control it, even when it offered a danger he might no longer be able to parry. Faced with Edward Carson at his trial, Wilde went for wit when he might have more wisely chosen a less urbane safety. Asked if he had ever kissed the youthful Walter Grainger, he indicated that he had not, and mentioned the young man's ugliness as a reason. The correct answer would have been that he had certainly not kissed him because he was male. Carson was on to this immediately and saw how the wit, in pursuing his witticism, had betrayed himself in the eyes of the law. Penal servitude followed. Wilde did at least survive in his fashion. Yeshua of Nazareth did not survive his own ordeal, or perhaps he did, if one follows the gospel narratives. The paradoxicality continues: if you wish to be a true son of God, get yourself executed in public as a common criminal. That's the way to heaven, boys, unlikely as it might seem to you and your Sunday School teacher.

IRONY: KINGDOM OF DISSONANCE.

SEMANTIC BILOCATION: IRONY insists that meaning is never univocal in modernity (was it ever in antiquity?), and all situations are overdetermined rather than determined — that is, there is always a manifold of causes, which cannot be ultimately disentangled. When Kafka read a story like 'Metamorphosis' to his friends, we are told they could not stop laughing. They seem to have been inhabiting an avenue of irony which has subsequently been closed to us. Or perhaps we are missing the point that the first thing Gregor does in the story is to dream. And when reason sleeps, as Goya told us, it brings forth monsters.

The Sermon on the Mount is an essay in irony on an epic scale. If all the reversals of expectation mentioned are to be fulfilled, then…the Kingdom of Heaven is the antithesis of this world.

The Sermon on the Mount is an essay in irony on an epic scale. If all the reversals of expectation mentioned are to be fulfilled, then this can only be true if what Yeshua called the Kingdom of Heaven is the antithesis of this world. Blessed are the poor, though they seldom feel particularly blessed here themselves. In truth they can only truly be blessed once they are transposed to the Kingdom. This is presumably by means of death. The forces of law and order here will not be facilitating any promotion into felicity. As Bob Dylan put it: 'The cops here don't need you, and man they expect the same.' They are the forces of law and order, to be sure, but they like to keep both the law and the order all to themselves. You will need to look elsewhere for your own.

The silent chorus that the ironist appeals to already knows the worst; it's been there, seen that. Think for a moment of precisely who that 'you' is in Dylan's line. It is presumed that this 'you' will understand, or the song is in vain. Or take for example Thomas Love Peacock in *Nightmare Abbey*: 'The lovers were torn asunder, weeping and vowing everlasting constancy; and, in three weeks after this tragical event, the lady was led a smiling bride to the altar, by the Honourable Mr Lackwit; which is neither strange nor new.' Who is it who finds these reversals, disappointments and rearrangements neither strange nor new? Certainly not the lovers themselves. It is the ancient silent chorus, the ironic gathering at the back of the stage of those that know. What is it that they (or we) know? Everything – but particularly the darker aspects of everything.

A certain irony has often been remarked in literary history. Wilfred Owen, that passionate versifier of the horrors of life in the trenches on the Western Front, was killed in action on the fourth of November 1919, precisely one week, almost to the hour, before the

Armistice ended hostilities. He was promoted to Lieutenant the day after his death. Is this ironic? Only if Fate is a contriver of structural ironies, who employs biographical material so as to taunt us with reversals and disappointments. Only if Fate is in league with those casual gods whom Gloucester mentions in *Lear*, the ones who kill us for their sport.

Whether the ironist elects himself, or has irony thrust upon him, is perhaps an open question. One thing is not open to question: in the Kingdom of Dissonance, dissonance must be registered precisely or it will issue as mere cacophony. And the ironist could easily insist that his ultimate justification is this: life itself presents us all with an ironic dilemma. We wish to live and are condemned to die. We crave happiness and fulfilment and are denied both. Our instincts must be repressed for the sake of civilization; its discontents are inseparable from its notable achievements. So, as we pine away in our sundry neurotic illnesses, we can hardly help but note the irony of being 'civilized'. And as we saw, Darwin argued that to get here at all we had to fulfil the requirements of what Coleridge called that 'blind Ideot called Nature'. Irony here is not a mere stylistic option. It is the expression of an intelligence confronted with injustice, or a cosmic asymmetry cockeyed enough to raise either an eyebrow or a smile.

Irony can also be a gesture of stylish exhaustion faced with what Harold Bloom calls our condition of belatedness. As Dylan sings elsewhere: 'You know it's all been done before. It's all been written in the Book.' And Thomas Mann in *Doctor Faustus* recounts how one modern composer sold his soul to the devil rather than be forever entrapped in inescapable repetition. Why do it at all, if it's all been done before? Why choose a career as a mere stylistic *pasticheur*?

What then would be the price of originality? It must have a moral cost.

IF STYLE IS the man, then an analysis of the style should lead us to the heart of the moralist and his matter. Modern physics discovered that nature itself may not be ironic, but it is undoubtedly paradoxical. A particle, viewed from a different angle, is a wave; and a wave, seen differently, is a particle. Niels Bohr was the formulator of this notion of complementarity. His own writing is engagingly clumsy, parenthetic, recursive. Every statement implies its own possible refutation. A great truth, he said, is one whose opposite is also true. And this truth is both discovered and enunciated in the morphology of his own style. In an intriguing parallel, the ironist can show us an entire scene in particle mode, then switch lenses and equations, and show us the same scene portrayed as waves. The shift in point of view changes the content, and then what was the same is no longer the same.

There is a localised irony, directed towards a specified theatre of engagement. Such irony is confident that there is a larger context which can quell this specific problem. Churchill faced with a mandarin civil servant whose grandeur of expression did not escape pomposity, famously wrote: 'this is the kind of writing up with which I will not put.' This is the irony that permits an adjustment that would in turn subsequently obviate the need for the irony. So the irony has now served its purpose, and the civil servant stops despatching his absurd stylistic injunctions. But when Swift writes *A Tale of a Tub*, the disturbance to be quelled is not local; in fact it begins to seem universal. This is the irony that finds an irremediable dissonance between the expectations of justice and the observation of continuing reality. If that dissonance is comprehensive enough, then it becomes what philosophers call infinitised irony.

Sometimes in Wilde, the ironic device became a mere reflex action. It could be altogether too happy to remain on the surface. It rearranged the lexical components while leaving the syntax intact: 'Work is the curse of the drinking classes.' Thus did the verbal ironies of his trial become the bitter irony of his imprisonment. Evelyn Waugh deployed irony as the necessary distance which the functioning human intelligence had to maintain from any comprehensive scheme of human improvement for the betterment of this world. One had to be careful to distinguish between the possibilities of this world, and those promises to be redeemed in the next. In his greatest work this device permits him the necessary distance from his subject matter that in turn facilitates the ironist's precision. But it can become a mere affectation, that famous ear-trumpet pointed towards a world he no longer wished to listen to in any case. At the time of the 1959 General Election, Waugh was asked by *The Spectator* how he might cast his vote. He said he did not presume to advise his Sovereign regarding her choice of ministers. This is an ironic periphrasis signifying: I can't see the point in voting for any of those fellows, frankly.

Irony can sometimes simply represent incongruity, and the comic effect of such juxtaposition. This can be effected in a simple rhyme. Eliot writes:

The crouched Brazilian jaguar
Compels the scampering marmoset
With subtle effluence of cat;
Grishkin has a maisonette…

Here the conjunction of *marmoset* and *maisonette* indicates the collision of two worlds. But the matter grows graver. And the disappointed justice with which irony so often tries to parley can overwhelm ironic resource. Faced with the reality of Hitler, the great Viennese ironist Karl Kraus simply said he could find nothing to say. Decades later, Tom Lehrer stopped writing and performing satirical songs. When asked why, he said it was difficult to be amusing about Vesuvius when you were currently living in Pompeii. That was during the presidency of Richard Nixon. Henry Kissinger had just been given the Nobel Peace Prize. Sometimes the ironist cannot keep pace with the realities he faces, let alone outrun them.

The Nazi authorities in Vienna finally let Freud go, but insisted he sign a document to the effect that they had not mistreated him. He signed and added this comment: *Ich kann die Gestapo jedermann auf das beste empfehlen*. 'I can recommend the Gestapo most highly to everyone.'

ZEUGMA IS ONE of the most characteristic tropes of irony, because zeugma enacts a doubleness, a forked effect which produces a dissonance. 'First you show me your heart, then you show me the door.' The single verb commands two different linguistic functions. The ironist would say that zeugma is appropriate to the ironic style precisely because of its veracity: it enunciates a truth about our situation, and about that figure of *Anthropos*, the same egregious figure who used to be described by the church fathers as *incurvatus in se*, turned back upon himself, doubled-up and self-contradicted. See how swiftly we flick between literal truth and metaphor. Thus does the ironist inhabit an ironic dilemma. Unable to find a domicile in any singular meaning on offer, he is also tormented by that subjective negativity which produces (and is produced by) such semantic and therefore philosophical homelessness.

In Schlegel's terminology, no affirmation is separable from its negation…One wants out of this dilemma, but the exit has been blocked.

In Schlegel's terminology, no affirmation is separable from its negation. And vice versa. The opposite of a great truth is also a truth. One wants out of this dilemma, but the exit has been blocked. Kierkegaard's leap beckons, as perhaps does Leonard Cohen's sojourns in certain Buddhist monasteries. Or even a life of action, for those who still have enough vigour left to make that possible. As Marianne Moore puts it: 'Blessed is the man/who does not sit in the seat of the scoffer/the man who does not denigrate, depreciate, denunciate…' Perhaps the man who has given up on any of the easier ironies too. Either give it to me straight or keep the gift entirely for yourself.

Socrates stays balanced and ironic to the end; his attitude to death seems, in the fullest sense of the word, philosophical. He had reached a fair old age by the standards of his time, and had lived a pretty rackety life. The wine appeared to be inseparable from the dialectics. Maybe he was ready to go. Perhaps he reckoned he had already asked enough questions. Time to let Plato get on with his scribbling for posterity. Would this be an irony? Or what if we were to discover a document that seemed to show, incontrovertibly, that Yeshua at the Last Supper had been asked what was to become of him now. In answer he had taken a piece of bread and said, 'This is my body'. He had then taken a cup of wine and said, 'This is my blood'. Then he had consumed both. And they had all understood. Just as he had consumed the bread and wine, so the Roman State would shortly consume him. What has been taken as the institution of the sacrament had in fact been an exercise in instrumental symbolism. Though this still leaves an opening for Emmaus. Once more he breaks the bread and pours the wine, as if to say: that which is consumed may still return, in order to be consumed again. If there is an irony here, it is a little shy in identifying itself. It is noteworthy that two of the greatest ironists who ever lived, Socrates and Yeshua of Nazareth, never seem to have written down a word, except for those fragments of lexis fingered in the dust as the woman taken in adultery was being accused. And those traces were kicked over immediately after.

A semantic vagrant then, a philosophical refugee, the ironist may be surrounded by meanings, but he cannot make a permanent home in any of them. He may be pushed into dialectics, and forced to accept that between this meaning and that one lies the shadow, and it inevitably blocks out the sun. He may be pushed into satire, where irony turns savage. He might even take some comfort from Bohr's *Principle of Complementarity*: modern physics has established that even nature would appear to be in two minds about itself. Sometimes the ironic scenario as presented to us might seem merely trite, little more than a cheap duplicity, like the tricking of Malvolio in *Twelfth Night*. Surely we have better things to do than this? And as for cosmic irony, shouldn't the cosmos have something better to do as well? Is the only difference between impersonal and cosmic irony one of scale? In the meantime the ironic stylist, so long as he does not succumb to the temptation of silence, continues to choose words with the greatest possible care. Malone in Beckett's novel *Malone Dies* reckons he is close to death, but thinks he might survive Saint John the Baptist's Day and even the Fourteenth of July. 'Indeed I would not put it past me to pant on to the Transfiguration, not to speak of the Assumption.' You have to smile. At the same time we recall Kent's words at the end of *Lear*: 'Is this the promised end?' The question is of course ironic, and Kent indicates that he himself will not be spending too much longer in this world. So should our ironic dilemmas prove terminal enough, we will not necessarily all die laughing.

IRONY AND AMITY.

THE ANONYMOUS REVIEWER in the *TLS* in 1907 spoke of Conrad's 'friendly irony' in *The Secret Agent*. Is it really friendly though, unless the phrase was intended like 'friendly fire', a term that would be brought into existence only a decade later in the Great War? The bullets and shells might have grinning faces painted on them, but they tear you to pieces, all the same. There are moments, it is true, where the irony might seem friendly, if still a little grim. Inspector Heat speaks of the anarchists being like fish moving through the sea of London, and when we encounter Comrade Ossipon, we are presumably meant to notice that his name might have started as the French for fish, *poisson*, before the entropic forces he champions broke the word down into its present curious mangle. His name is orthographically entropic. There is a certain playfulness too when Mr Vladimir asks Verloc what he thinks of 'having a go at astronomy'. It sounds innocent enough, in its cosmic weirdness, until we realise that what is being discussed is the bombing of the Greenwich Observatory, an explosive device aimed lethally at the First Meridian. This is the whimsicality of the terrorist, and it leads to Stevie's hideous death.

Modern London has provided the ironist with incalculable ironies. Eliot in *The Waste Land* lamented that the nymphs had departed the Thames. He notes that they have left in their wake the used prophylactics of the privileged children of the City. In comparison the London ironies of Wodehouse seem positively Edenic, the ironic whole being based upon this central structural irony: all the intelligence and knowledge lie with the servant, but the money and possessions remain for ever in the hands of the witless master.

In 1965 in a gallery in Düsseldorf, Josef Beuys covered his face with honey and gold leaf and spoke at great length to a dead hare he cradled in his arms. He said that it was much easier to talk to the hare about paintings (even post-mortem) than humans, crippled as they were by their stubborn rationality. This is an irony soaked through with tragedy, and there was something of Lear in Beuys' enactment. By the time we reach Jeff Koons though, we are in the postmodern culture of the piss-take; which is to say, irony as parody, where all gravities are swallowed with a yawn. His jovial returns upon the theme of carnal love manage to turn the human body itself into a form of kitsch, a multi-coloured confection to be consumed until nausea at last interferes. Here we seem to be in the realm of Bill Baillie's postmodern vegetarian, who eats meat, but only ironically.

But back to that review of 1907. How friendly can irony ever be? It can be urbane, certainly, but urbanity is not necessarily friendly; it is frequently the means of maintaining courtesy in the total absence of any real amity whatsoever.

All irony is a form of aggression: the ironist shakes an observed world into defamiliarization, as if it were a snowglobe.

Conrad himself in a letter to Cunningham Grahame insisted that there were no 'malicious intentions' in his portrayal of the anarchists. One can easily imagine a letter from Swift to Pope insisting that he harboured no ill will towards the Yahoos. All irony is a form of aggression: the ironist shakes an observed world into defamiliarization, as if it were a snowglobe. The fact is that Conrad's portrayal of the seditious London brotherhood is uniformly negative. There is barely a redeeming feature to be shared out amongst them. And they are all (despite some curious and dubious genealogical claims by Verloc) foreign. Amidst this bunch of nihilistic misfits, sponges and layabouts, there is not a single British heart-of-oak. And that elegant sponsor of murder and mayhem, Mr Vladimir of the Embassy, is undoubtedly Russian. Conrad harboured no sentimentalities regarding Russia or the Russians. But 'friendly irony'?

There are more ironies in *The Secret Agent* than it is easy to count, sometimes several on a single page, but the overarching irony is expressed not through any particular statement or relationship, but in the pervasive imagery. Lurking behind this narrative were some of the more recent preoccupations of science, and of the general public: the heat death of the sun and the Law of Entropy. The Second Law of Thermodynamics had recently brought home the dreadful truth that all systems ultimately degenerate to a maximum state of disorganization; that energy always degrades and scatters. We lose some in its higher form of organization every time we employ it. The imagery of the book contrasts darkness and cold with light and heat. The chief protagonist of law and order is, after all called Chief Inspector Heat, a name as pointedly allegorical as any in Dickens. As we saw, he sometimes thinks of the anarchists out on the street as being like fish in the darkness of the sea. As does the Assistant Commissioner: 'His descent into the street was like the descent into a slimy aquarium from which the water had been run off. A murky, gloomy dampness enveloped him...He might have been but one more of the queer foreign fish that can be seen of an evening about there flitting round the dark corners.'

Verloc himself, double agent between the forces of law and order and those of anarchy, is a biographical exemplum of the entropic principle: he starts in a state of order and moves into disorder: 'Born of industrious parents for a life of toil, he had embraced indolence from an impulse as profound, as inexplicable and as imperious as the impulse which directs a man's preference for one particular woman in a given thousand.' That is entropy in its human form.

Knowledge introduces us to entropy. Only ignorance can give us the illusion that the sun will never die; that warmth and light will be our lot for ever.

His wife Winnie moves from ignorance to knowledge, and thereby from placidity to murderousness. Knowledge here is an entry into the darkness and cold. Knowledge introduces us to entropy. Only ignorance can give us the illusion that the sun will never die; that warmth and light will be our lot for ever. Her ultimate act in regard to Verloc is to make sure the light outside him is turned off, just as she had so recently turned out the light (however dim) that had shone inside him. Her ultimate act in regard to herself is to depart the light and warmth above the earth for the dark and cold beneath the waves. She throws herself overboard from the cross-Channel steamer. That queer and mangled fish, Ossipon, had helped seal her final despair.

But it is poor Stevie who is the truly emblematic figure of human entropy. He is tormented by any form of pain, inflicted either on humans or animals. And his utter devotion to the goodness of his sister's husband leads to him being blown to pieces by the explosive device he is carrying; he is hoist with his own petard. Led to his death by that Verloc whom he has been raised to revere, he is disintegrated and has to be gathered up with a shovel. But like Humpty Dumpty, no forces – however regal – will ever put him back together again.

At the end the Professor is still free to walk the streets with his own explosive device concealed about his person. He is an explosion waiting to happen, a remarkably proleptic portrayal of the modern suicide bomber. All human ingenuity has culminated in this threat to human order and well-being. And this was seven years before humanity started blowing itself to bits on the Western and Eastern Fronts.

The structural irony in which the narrative situates itself is that grand construction of (mis)perception whereby the reader – along with Winnie – imagines that Mr Verloc has blown himself to smithereens when in fact he has instead made the arrangements whereby Stevie blows himself to smithereens, thus turning Mrs Verloc, who thought it didn't do to look too deeply into things, first into a murderer, then a suicide. Conrad's irony is a recognition of homelessness. To that degree many of the first reviewers were right: this was indeed the vision of an alien, but his alienation had a cosmic perspective. He understood all too well how we mistake one another, and misconstrue our condition here on earth.

INTENTIONLESS IRONY.

THE PROBLEM OF usage and implication often arises, as we have seen, when we have an ironic effect without any ironic intention, whether impersonal or cosmic. The use of the word 'ironic' then becomes problematical, for how can there be an irony without an ironist? It is ironic, we say, that those people died of thirst and the following day the monsoon arrived. But then where might such irony actually subsist? On what plane? If this really were an irony in the full sense, an intended doubleness of meaning, where one plane of significance occludes the other before offering to reverse it, which agency is deploying the dual meaning? From whence is our bifocal epistemology originating? If, like Gloucester, we can say 'As flies to wanton boys are we to the gods/They kill us for their sport' then the irony can indeed be a full one: here is a lethal jokiness of fate for us to savour, even as it is being inflicted upon us. It is our misery which makes the gods smile. Or if like Jacques in *As You Like It* we can assert that 'All the world's a stage', then this image of the *theatrum mundi* can provide us with a framework of fateful display in which all ironic effects can ultimately be sourced as ironic intentions.

But without such a theatrical cosmology, we appear to be dealing with coincidences which produce ironic effects, but with no ironic intentions to motivate or dislocate them. Our use of the word 'ironic' then produces ironies in its turn; ironies of disconnection between a perceived effect and the dislocation from any meaningful causality that might have preceded it. This is an irony born entirely of contingency, and as such it has been severed from any rhetorical roots. It wasn't ironic that the monsoon arrived the next day; it was simply bad luck that it did not come a day earlier. If it were a genuine irony, then we humans would be more significant in the scheme of things than we really are. To report these matters truthfully, we need to be anti-ironic, as were many of the early stories of Ernest Hemingway, and much of the poetry of Hardy. To allow irony a place here is to delude ourselves that we have a more significant position in the ultimate scheme of creation than we in fact do.

Take a single example. In the University of Birmingham Library there is a curious item. It is a badly charred Bible. It is thought that this was the Bible from which Joseph Priestley read in the Unitarian meeting house he frequented in that city. The reason it is so badly burnt is that it found itself at the centre of the Church-and-King Riots in 1791. These same riots and their keenly patriotic rioters destroyed Priestley's laboratory, one of the finest in Europe at the time. Now Priestley was the discoverer of oxygen as a separate element in these islands (others were simultaneously discovering that same elementary singularity elsewhere), and he was a lifelong student of the processes of fire. If we say that the authentic stink of burning which still emits from that damaged piece of holy writ embodies an irony, given the nature of Priestley's chemical studies, then we are in effect saying that Clio, the goddess of history, must be deemed a zealous ironist in her own right. If we are not saying this, then we must presumably imply that irony can be solely a matter of effect, with no manner of intention anywhere in sight. No *theatrum mundi*, no playful gods smiling at human misery, no double-dealing Clio, merely a compound dissonance, a random effect, which elicits an ironic response in us. So the dissonance perceived lies not so much in the *materia* presented, which is merely discrete and coincidental, as in our concerted response to it. The irony lies in how we would have contrived matters differently, had the contrivance been in fact at our disposal. Such irony is not so much objective then, as *voulu*.

IRONY'S FOOTNOTE.

THE CHARACTERISTIC TEXTUAL manoeuvre of irony is for the words on the page to trip themselves up, then catch themselves sufficiently quickly that the meaning does not fall over so much as foreground itself, often in front of its own mirror image. The *eiron* stares across the stage at the *alazon*; understatement looks overstatement in the eye, and winks at the audience. The footnote can be the perfect means to this end, since the extended foot actually obtrudes itself at the bottom of the page, and the page can be seen to take a bit of a tumble over it. Pages can of course argue with themselves (and within themselves) in different ways. In the dialogue poems of Marvell and Yeats, the quarrel is conducted relatively straightforwardly. This feels like an overt pugilistic contest, employing Marquess of Queensberry rules, but there is something sneaky about the footnote. Often enough it does what the dwarves used to do at court: play the fool, extemporize the role of the licensed jester. Gibbon's footnotes in *Decline and Fall* permit him to be even more acidulous and rib-poking than he already is in the text. If you were an early Christian or theologian of note, you would not wish to be memorialized thus, buried in one of these neat little typographic coffins.

But still in Gibbon the textual footnote is playing the straight man to itself. Something different had happened with Swift and Pope. In *A Tale of A Tub* and *The Dunciad*, the footnote signs its own declaration of unilateral independence. In those works, the footnote is a space of riot and misrule. These notes are trapdoors in the textual stage through which you can fall, and there is no guarantee you will ever stop in your descent, since such footnotes provide a space for that infinitized irony that so alarms philosophers. It might have had its birth in Schlegel's exposition of irony, where the opposite must always be embraced. Certain words contain their own antonyms. Freud was fascinated by these, giving *cleave* as an example. We cleave in two, but we also cleave *unto*. This idea also finds a locus in Empson's seventh type of ambiguity, where opposites are held together, like cathodes and anodes, sharing the electric current between them. (Niels Bohr, we remember, after his study of wave/particle complementarity, believed that all great truths contained their opposites. In 1900 to say a particle might be a wave, or a wave become particulate, would have been a paradox, perhaps even an irony. After the Solvay Conference of 1927, it became the statement of a scientific fact.) We seem to end up inhabiting an irony so large it starts to appear inescapable, and sometimes even invisible; an irony without any unironized exterior peg by which it might ultimately secure itself.

And so we move on through Borges, whose footnotes provide exquisite points of scholarly reference, frequently quoting texts that only ever existed as facets of the author's invention. Or there is Nabokov's *Pale Fire*, where the notes so bully the text they are claiming to gloss and elucidate that there is in effect an undeclared war between primary text and pendant annotation. Finally we arrive at David Foster Wallace, for whom the footnote was a further site of alienation and paranoia, a mirror world of disputation and distortion, with no respite.

From being a necessary addition and explication to a classic text, the footnote started to act as though it were a sapper in the original meaning of that word: one engaged in undermining the foundations of a besieged citadel. The citadel here is of course the text itself, and every one of its pretensions to authority. The footnote insists that it should never be confused with that text, even expressing itself in a differently sized font.[1]

CHAPTER NOTE

1. Thus.

11.

Hell

AND ITS ABOLITIONS.

WHAT IS HELL? It is either a spiritual state or location, which is the domicile of demons and damned human souls, or it is a projection of the psychic darkness which exists inside the human imagination. In Roman Catholic churches there is an option whether the Nicene Creed is used in the service, or the Apostles' Creed. Only the latter declares that the Messiah was crucified and killed, and then 'descended into hell'. These days, in public worship, there is frequently an ellipsis where that harrowing might be spoken of. Often enough he is simply dead and buried, and the next line would inform you: 'On the third day he rose from the dead.'

The fact is that a great deal of western Christianity, in many of its public performances, has become nervous of propounding a God who could condemn anyone to eternal suffering. In modern terms it started to seem a little harsh, even for an omnipotently judging deity. So dare we hope that all may be saved, and even the demons too? Or, at worst, burn away to a cinder when confronted with the brightness of the light? That at least, if not the happiest of career moves for one enamoured of redemption, still sounds a better option than eternal damnation. One way of seeming to resolve the matter, frequently employed by subtle theologians, is to declare that there undoubtedly is a hell, but that there is not necessarily anyone in it. Which begs a questions, surely: what's it for, then? A hell without even Hitler or the Kommandant of Auschwitz starts to look like a football stadium without any goalposts, players or even a ball. Can it really be, in the formulation of post-war power-bloc politics, a credible deterrent? Could the Almighty have torn an ontological hole in the very fabric of being simply to make all intelligent beings think twice?

Everything is straightforward here only for those zealots for whom everything is always straightforward anyway. In *Paradise Lost*, Satan exhorts his fallen companions with this assertion:

> The mind is its own place, and of itself can make
> A heaven of hell, a hell of heaven.

THIS IS A specific heresy that for a while might have travelled under the name of *psychologism*. It was favoured, Alastair Fowler tells us in his magisterial notes to *Milton*, by Amaury de Bene. It should be distinguished from another heresy, propounded by Mephistopheles in Marlowe's *Doctor Faustus*: 'Why this is hell. Nor am I out of it.' That perversion of doctrine was for a time known as ubiquism. The first heresy asserts that hell is no more than a state of mind; so change your mind and you will find that you might well be in heaven. It's all psychological anyway. This seems remarkably close to certain self-help philosophies of our own day. Dale Carnegie reminded us in the invaluable *How to Win Friends and Influence People*: 'Two men looked out through prison bars/One saw mud and the other saw stars.' It's all a question of attitude, then. As for Satan, he is (understandably) trying to look on the bright side, given the way the war in heaven has finally turned out. One can't help but think of W. C. Fields: 'Been reading the Bible again today, looking for loopholes.'

The descent into, and the harrowing of, hell, still feature prominently in many liturgies, including the eastern orthodox variety, and their iconographic itineraries carry considerable force. By descending into hell, in one version of Jesus's Sabbatarian immolation, the Messiah goes to the lowest place in life and in the afterlife, and finally expresses his redemptive power even there. The metaphors of verticality appear unavoidable here. No one ever *ascends* into hell. Whenever Milton employs the word *ruin* he is always aware (astute etymologist that he was) that *ruinare* in the Latin means to fall or collapse. If Jesus is to assert his power throughout the whole of creation, then even hell must presumably require his grave sojourn. No zone of experience is to remain untouched. In one legalistic gloss, Satan wrongly claims Jesus as his sanctioned prisoner, assuming the Messiah has been justly imprisoned in the Prince of Evil's posthumous bailiwick, and then the injustice of this seizure of the one man after Adam who was ever entirely without sin, splits open the hermetically sealed gates of hell for ever. *Harrowing* is a breaking of the surface, whether of the field or of the carceral spaces of the Inferno. Once Jesus has accomplished his harrowing, the righteous dead (even though not entirely without sin themselves) can now at last be released. They troop out of Hades with Jesus in the vanguard, those old patricians and prophets: Abraham, Moses, Isaiah. One of the medieval mystery plays was entitled *The Harrowing of Hell*. In the version in the York Plays, Satan recognises Jesus. I know you, he says, you are the son of the wright (maker, carpenter perhaps) in Galilee. What's supposed to be so special about you then? One could describe the early Christian tradition as a lengthy attempt to answer Satan's question.

This is the domicile of those who have severed themselves from the source of any and every meaning.

There is also a more dramatic, and for modern tastes perhaps more psychologically convincing, version of what happened during that dead day between crucifixion and resurrection. This was described in various ways by the theologian Hans Urs von Balthazar, who was dependent in his turn on the visions of the mystic Adrienne Von Speyr. Jesus here is utterly cancelled, quite God-bereft, at the end of his experience on the cross. In the only words of Aramaic in the text, he expresses his abandonment thus: *Eloi, eloi, lama sabachtani?*, which is to say, My God, my God, why has thou forsaken me? This cancellation continues in his ultimate descent into the region of the hopeless, those who have freely renounced all communication with God. In this act of voluntary self-annihilation, Jesus enters into the anti-world of the negation of all meaningful experience. He accepts the vastation of meaning and value that constitutes damnation itself. This is the domicile of those who have severed themselves from the source of any and every meaning. The dead Jesus is here translated into the cosmic region of nullity. Thus does his redemptive power touch even that darkness, before he finally embarks on his ascent out of darkness once more into the light of redemptive meaning.

A number of papal bulls in the thirteenth and fourteenth centuries made the matter plain: you were either destined for heaven or hell. This is the *eschaton*, the final thing, that provides us with our eschatology. Purgatory becomes a staging-post for those destined for salvation. But the four last things, as spelt out in the catechism, are these: death, judgment, heaven and hell. Purgatory was a relatively late invention, and one which the reformers saw fit to abolish, as a papist superstition, which led inevitably to those degraded forms of negotiation with the Almighty represented by Brother Tetzel and his sale of indulgences, in order to finance the building of Saint Peter's. So we all have one destination or the other. The obverse and the reverse of all our destinies carry only two names: heaven or hell. Pursue the matter vigorously, and you will still frequently find this belief articulated in Roman Catholic pronouncements. But Jesus's descent into hell has managed to vanish from much of the western liturgy, as it is publicly uttered. It appears to have become one of those truths better left unsaid. Times have certainly changed since Dante.

JEFFREY BURTON RUSSELL, in his multi-volume study of Satan[1] points out that there are only four world religions that have ever had a Devil; many more have demons, but the notion of a singular embodiment of the principle of transcendent evil is restricted to this quaternity: Zoroastrianism (or Mazdaism); ancient Judaism, though not the modern variety; Christianity and Islam. By propounding an agent of darkness and destruction set over against the divine will, any creed lays itself open to the charge of dualism.

This has become a lethal insult in theological or philosophical discourse, though it is worthy of note that there is no satisfactory antonym to dualism here. What is the alternative to a dualistic or binary view that finds a struggle between forces of light and forces of darkness? Holism? That doesn't sound right, somehow, hinting at homemade sandals and dark proteinaceous bread. Monism? That feels tricky too. The problem with any monistic solution here is that the darkness will presumably have to be situated inside God Himself; otherwise from whence precisely did it arise? Well, Milton has Chaos, out of which all is made, and this allows for the possibility that there is something unregenerate in it which will not quite be coaxed into redemptiveness. Burton Russell highlights the problem with a picture of a limestone sculpture of Quetzalcoatl, on one side the creative god of life and on the other a skull-faced bringer of death and destruction. Obverse and reverse here appear to overcome the dilemma of dualism; or do they merely foreground it?

Christian orthodoxy has tended to favour a strand of thought going back through Aquinas to Augustine: the *privatio boni*. On this basis everything created is good; what ends up as evil is privation or warping into negativity of that which was initially wholesome. So, Satan starts off as Lucifer, the lightbearer, the brightest of the seraphim. It is his sin through pride which corrupts that glorious being into the most inglorious agent of all. But this notion of evil as pure negativity generates its own problems. Evil can be proactive, programmatic, remarkably forceful. It is hard to see where all this energy comes from, out of pure privation.

This tempts some thinkers towards simplification, even vulgarisation. In a recent issue of the *London Review of Books*, Terry

Eagleton said of Brian Levack's book *The Devil Within* that 'it could do with a touch more theology'.[2] He then went on to say: 'Satan is the image of Yahweh as judge and patriarch – as an irascible prima donna of a God who needs to be kept sweet. Jesus, by contrast, is the image of God as lover, comrade and counsel for the defence.' This exhibits that characteristic breeziness which seems to endear this writer to so many. But given the twinning of the word *image* here, and the link to Jesus, Eagleton appears to assume that Satan can be seen as an 'aspect' of God. He cannot. The tradition, to be sure, is befogged with confusions, misprisions and dubious etymologies. Lucifer the light-bearer arises out of Isaiah, who would seem to have been apostrophizing Nebuchadnezzar at the time, as the son of the morning, now 'fallen from heaven'. This is what will subsequently provide the association of the word *Lucifer* with the morning or evening star, Venus. The church fathers, including Jerome, often employed this nomenclature.

SATAN THE ADVERSARY makes appearances in many of the books of Hebrew scripture, including Numbers, Job, Chronicles, Psalms and Zechariah. In most of these instances, the figure portrayed is an angel filling an office, most certainly not an 'aspect of God', as Shekinah can be seen as an aspect or manifestation of the Almighty. Nor is this angelic personage in any way fallen, a notion unknown to Hebrew scripture. In New Testament times the confusion begins in earnest; it never goes away. Dante, Chaucer and Milton are all confident that Lucifer is the name of the great light-bearer in heaven, but after his rebellion he becomes Satan for ever after. There is no scriptural warrant for this.

Satan, according to the Talmud, was created on the sixth day of Creation. He was usually thought, as we have said, to be the head of the seraphim. Seraphim, the highest order of angels, had six wings, but Satan is often portrayed with twelve. In the *Summa*, Thomas Aquinas insisted that Satan must have been of the cherubim. This insistence he based on the false etymology which claimed that the word cherubim was derived from knowledge, and was therefore compatible with mortal sin. He contrasted one false etymology with another, which derived the word seraphim from charity, an attribute he believed incompatible with mortal sin.

'Angels are bright still, though the brightest fell' we are told in *Macbeth*. And the notion of the brightest angel of all who then becomes ruler of the darkest kingdom starts to play its part in New Testament texts and polemics. It features in subsequent Christian art, literature and music, right through to the present day. The darkest and most potent leader of the damned is often hybridised with ancient figures like Pluto, who also ruled the realms below and liked to gather up unsuspecting humans for infernal purposes. The extent of this fallen angel's power has provided a lengthy and confusing intellectual tradition, in which can be traced a struggle between monism and dualism in Christian thought through the centuries.

Walter Benjamin was fond of recalling a particularly specialised genus of angels whose sole function was to come into being, chant halleluiahs to the Almighty, then promptly disappear into the angelic black hole Providence had prepared for them. But even they exhibited free will. Even these ephemerids of the angelic orders weren't simply aspects of God, employing preternatural smoke and mirrors in order to let Yahweh congratulate himself on being so splendiferous.

It is possible to read the Satan of Numbers as a periphrasis for Yahweh, but once we enter the post-Exilic period, we are dealing with an independent supernatural being. From this point on, whatever else he is, Satan can only be regarded as an image or aspect of God by certain Gnostic creeds, and by Satanists. And of course by Terry Eagleton, whose prodigious flow is rarely halted by fastidious scruple.

WHAT EXACTLY THE Jesus of the gospels meant by the fires of judgment, and by ultimate condemnation, is a matter for ceaseless debate. 'The Gehenna of fire' seems to be as close to his actual words as we are likely to get, and that refers us to the civic dump outside Jerusalem, Gehenna by name, linking back to the Valley of Hinnom, the origin of which is unknown, but it is possible that it was once a place of human sacrifice, dedicated perhaps to Moloch. More informally and subsequently, it seems to become a place where rubbish was incinerated. That allows for the notion of simply ceasing to be, in a final puff of smoke. But other gospel passages and parables insist on continued suffering as the price of disregarding the will of God. That will soon transmute into 'eternal punishment and suffering' in the Christian tradition. And once Christianity seizes on the idea of a place of eternal suffering, and the busy grinning demons that are its grim wardens, it is very reluctant to let go. Shrieking devils with tridents represent a more vigorous iconography than seraphically smiling angels with harps. We might all prefer to live in Mr Brownlow's house in *Oliver Twist*, but we undoubtedly prefer reading about Bill Sikes as he eyes up Nancy for her final beating. Even in the surrealist landscapes of Hieronymous Bosch, God the Father in the *Garden of Eden* looks like a disconsolate Welsh preacher on a wet Sunday, whereas hell is where all the life is. Nothing damp and disconsolate about Bosch's demons; they rage excitedly. Exactly the same pattern is repeated in *Paradise Lost*.

James Joyce in *A Portrait of the Artist as a Young Man* cobbles together his own damnation sermon during the retreat which Stephen Dedalus attends. It is not a copy of any single sermon, but it rings true in its grisly imaginings. Generations of Catholics had a very dim sense of heaven, but a sense of hell so viciously potent that it was psychically ineradicable. In many of the great buildings of Christianity (the cathedral at Pisa, for example) the portrayal of damnation is somewhat more absorbing than the portrayal of salvation. Most readers prefer Dante's *Inferno* to his *Paradiso*. Everyone prefers *Paradise Lost* to *Paradise Regained*. And if this is so, we might pause for a moment and wonder why. If the non-believer insists that hell is a projection out of the darkness of the human psyche, neither more nor less, then we must come to a melancholy conclusion: the amount of darkness within us appears to be infinite in dimension. There is at least as much darkness inside us as there is light outside. So where precisely does that leave us?

Two notable twentieth century artists went out of their way to re-instate hell at the centre of their work: T. S. Eliot and Francis Bacon. There is even a triptych of Bacon's which is named after an unfinished dramatic work of Eliot's, *Sweeney Agonistes*. (We should note that the title of this work was not provided by Bacon himself, but by the Marlborough Gallery, after Bacon had informed them that he had been reading that text of Eliot's while painting his triptych.) Eliot came to believe that the greatest poet of the last thousand years was Dante, and that the greatest modern equivalent to him was Baudelaire. Both of these masters, we might note, were much preoccupied with hell. As Eliot abandoned the vestiges of his youthful Unitarianism, a religion as indifferent to the notion of damnation as it is to the concept of the Trinity, he found an undoubted comfort in a doctrinal position that included the choice of eternal damnation as the ultimate expression of human freedom. He had no time for versions of Christianity which sought to abolish hell, accusing one interlocutor of trying to turn God into Santa Claus.

It is easy to forget now that the *Inferno* of Dante was regarded with horror by many in the nineteenth century, as a relic of that medieval superstition...

It is easy to forget now that the *Inferno* of Dante was regarded with horror by many in the nineteenth century, as a relic of that medieval superstition which modern churchmen had repaired at last with their more enlightened views. Dante Gabriel Rossetti translated parts of the *Inferno* into English (his grandfather had translated all of *Paradise Lost* into Italian), and there were versions produced throughout the Victorian age, before Binyon's magisterial version in the early twentieth century. But such a vision of hell, of eternal suffering, vouchsafed by the poetic imagination, made people uneasy. All those visions of hell appeared so antiquated; they belonged to another age. Perhaps the most brilliant critique of the *Inferno* of Victorian times was *Alice's Adventures in Wonderland*. Here we have an infernal realm without any real infernal powers. The Reverend Charles Dodgson did not believe in hell. He kept quiet about it elsewhere, since it was still the official doctrine of the

Anglican faith, even if it was starting to gather a certain amount of dust in the theological muniments room.

Whatever Dodgson might have thought, Eliot did not believe in a Christianity without hell; it smacked of that Unitarian smudging of boundaries which had come to so appal him. Emersonian self-reliance; the making of one's own paradise: he was having none of that. He often referred to such intellectual manoeuvres as 'liberalism'. His work often portrays quite specific infernos, little side-chapels to the nave's great theme. *Sweeney Agonistes*, the unfinished drama that so intrigued Bacon, is set in a kind of hell on earth, with Sweeney reminiscing about his friend who 'did a girl in'; we are left reasonably convinced that the murderer must have been Sweeney himself. But the vision of life in death that he conjures seems no worse (and a great deal more real) than the social rounds of fake joy and spurious bonhomie that the London of the time has on offer, in the social life celebrated by the other characters in the drama. One can find a curious parallel to *Sweeney Agonistes* in the film *In Bruges*, which also has people reminiscing about those they have killed, and also seeking momentary pleasure in seemingly hellish conditions. Both are dramas of confinement; in both cases the places of confinement are arenas of damnation. These are infernal translations, as are Bacon's silently screaming figures inside their vestigial cages and cells.

BLAKE HAD BEEN commissioned to illustrate Dante in the last year of his life, and he said something of the greatest relevance here: that Dante's *Inferno* was real, not despite the fact that it was imagined, but because of it. Nothing is real that is not fully imagined. Blake himself seemed to feel that hell and the demons were a projection of the human mind when in thrall to that most invidious of all human projections: Old Nobodaddy (*aka* God). That appears to be his argument three decades before in *The Marriage of Heaven and Hell*. He himself did not believe there was any such place or state as hell, where the sinful were eternally punished. Nevertheless, he was in no doubt of the reality of Dante's vision. And he once saw the Devil on the stairs, and subsequently drew him. He found the experience fearful.

So we have a curiosity worthy of remark. One believer, Eliot, and one unbeliever, Bacon, situated the infernal experience at the very centre of their art. Whatever theology might have to say on the subject, the imagination insisted on retaining the kingdom of the damned. Eliot was unrelenting in his seriousness regarding damnation. He roundly told off his old friend Ezra Pound for the latter's 'Hell Cantos' (XIV-XV). What you have created, he said, is a hell for other people, and that makes it unreal. It is a mechanism for denunciation, not the terrifying place of dark spiritual realities envisioned by Dante. Make it real, he told Pound: put me in your hell, then it will be real. Sweeney in *Sweeney Agonistes*, and Harry in *The Family Reunion*, are real and compelling precisely because we sense so much of Eliot in them.

Those entirely enamoured of the version of Eliot's first marriage propounded in the play and film *Tom and Viv* should read Ronald Schuchard's *Eliot's Dark Angel*. Eliot went through his own version of hell, that's for sure. And it was while undergoing it that he realised the importance of Dante and Baudelaire, and the necessity in his imagination, most of all his religious imagination, for there to be a place of ultimate damnation, to secure the realities of human experience at all. Otherwise there was nothing serious in mortality. In attempting to parenthesize hell, Macbeth and his wife end up trapped inside that same sealed parenthesis: they have locked themselves into the earthly hell that is now their castle and their lives. In fact, their castle becomes one of the most powerful recuperations of the claustrophobia of Dante's *Inferno* in western literature. Why this is hell; nor are we out of it.

The comic and the cartoon have become so central to our culture that we are entitled to ask a question: can hell be meaningfully represented within them? We should note that in Tex Avery-style cartoons – the *Loony Tunes* school – there is no death, and there is no hell. However appalling the catastrophe, Tom getting run over by a steam-roller, say, the character will finally rise up from the asphalt, shake himself free of his stigmata, and walk off towards the next adventure. Tex Avery's world is one of universal redemption, where we may not only hope that all men may be saved, but all cats, mice, budgerigars and road runners too. Not so in Disney. Disney films have death at their hearts, and a menacing sense of evil, which requires real moral and physical courage to overcome. The fire in the forest kills your mother; the treacherous enemies kill your father. Disney's is a complex moral world, and the evil characters are truly evil. They pass one of the crucial tests of the representation of evil: the ability to generate childhood nightmares.

BUT NOW A most curious phenomenon has come to visit: the comic book world of supermen and spidermen, batmen and spacemen, has returned with full moral force in the form of the graphic novel. And one of the most potent preoccupations of the graphic novel is evil and damnation. There is now a highly acclaimed graphic novel version of *The Inferno*, using Doré's images. And there is also, unavoidably, *From Hell*, the graphic novel by Alan Moore and Eddie Campbell, which explores the world of Jack the

Ripper, and the East End of London in which his appalling (and unsolved) crimes were committed. The streets of Whitechapel are portrayed as a version of hell, monochromatic, overwhelmed with darkness, both physical and moral. Dickens often portrayed them that way too; so did Conan Doyle in *The Sign of the Four*. Baudelaire saw Paris as a vision of hell, though occasionally of paradise too. Walter Benjamin said that capitalism, in the capital city, was an infernal phantasmagoria, whose only antidote to hellish repetition was fashion.

As for the comic format, in one sense it might be closer to Shakespeare's theatre than the printed book without illustrations. After all, when you watched Shakespeare, you saw scene after scene, with figures (frequently caricatural in gesture, and thereby troubling Hamlet) making their utterances, and then disappearing from the frame. Just the same with a comic novel. John Berger once criticised Francis Bacon for creating cartoons of tortured images; he compared some of Bacon's tortured figures in highlighted frames to Disney. He was to return to this theme in a later essay. There he said he had been wrong: Bacon did indeed use the caricatural form of cartoon images for his painting, often all too vividly aware of the frame in which they were imprisoned, but it was that which gave the work its strength. Berger admitted he had previously missed the point.

The images in *From Hell* are beautifully drawn. The visual world conveyed is remarkably convincing. Looming out of the Victorian world of London are the extraordinary structures of Nicholas Hawksmoor's churches, and the hermetic designs they are sometimes supposed to have imposed upon London. Here we need to pause for a moment. Nicholas Hawksmoor and his London churches have become the centre of a certain dark concentration. Now, the churches are weirdly distinctive, and Hawksmoor (a Mason like his master Wren) was known as the devil's architect, because of a fondness for incorporating pagan and hermetic details into his buildings. But the great leap into the dark regarding him came in 1975 with the publication by Iain Sinclair of *Lud Heat*. This work, in verse and prose, contains the essay: 'Hawksmoor, His Churches'. This appears to make the claim that the five significant London churches constructed by Nicholas Hawksmoor figure a pentacle over the city; that they shape a hermetic design which focuses dark energies in specific parts (specific moments) of the city. Sinclair even provides us with a diagram so we can see the uncanny urban geometry he is adumbrating. It should be pointed out immediately that Hawksmoor did not choose his sites: they were assigned to him. And Sinclair seems to have become a little less literal about this diagrammatic purposiveness of the siting of Hawksmoor's churches of late. The configuration has effectively become metaphoric.

But there it was now, situated in the psyche of our myriad students of psychic darkness, and there it has remained. Peter Ackroyd wrote *Hawksmoor* in the shadow of Sinclair's psychogeographic mappings, and *From Hell* follows suit. The thesis here is that Sir William Gull, Queen Victoria's physician, sets out on a mission to remove the sources of a threat to the throne: certain women, all of whom are on the game, who know that Prince Albert (Eddie) has fathered a child with a Roman Catholic woman, and has even married the mother. This could undoubtedly represent a threat to the throne, and Gull takes it upon himself to execute all of them, using masonic butchery, and his own considerable anatomical knowledge. All the senior police figures of the time are on the square (Masons), as is Gull himself, and a certain amount of connivance goes on, but Gull still takes it upon himself, as they would say in the army, to exceed his authority. His trusted coachman Netley is in on it, since he has to set up the assignations and then remove the perpetrator to safety immediately afterwards. Netley has a stab at maintaining his humanity by vomiting copiously, but he does his duty by his masonic master all the same. And the master is convinced he is operating within the hermetic shadows of the Hawksmoor pentacle. These are killings performed for a higher destiny. Jack the Ripper is securing the future of the kingdom.

The title comes from one of Jack's rare communications, which is signed as emitting 'from hell'. So once again we are situated in infernal darkness, this time on the streets of London in 1888. Moore is a shrewd and non-simplifying writer. He concludes about the Jack the Ripper killings that we cannot in truth come to a conclusion about them. We are obliged to construct a fiction in which certain of the facts may achieve concord; that is as far as we can go. In this he is with the Don DeLillo of *Libra*, and against the Oliver Stone of *JFK*, where Jim Garrison's final lengthy speech explains everything that happened in Texas that day in 1963. DeLillo has called such comprehensive explanation a form of nostalgia; nostalgia for the overarching narrative which can situate every last little fact in its explanatory schema. *Libra* concludes that we will never know all that happened regarding the assassination of JFK; and *From Hell* seems to come to a similar conclusion regarding Jack the Ripper. The only thing we can be certain of is that some great evil was taking place among us. Certain urban spaces were metamorphosing into hell.

We are left, for better or worse, with our own fascination with the infernal. Why are we so imaginatively enamoured of the darkness? What is it about *The Exorcist* that cinema audiences (*videlicit* ourselves) still find so compelling? The book, which was written by William Peter Blatty, who also scripted the film, had been based originally on 'an actual case of possession and exorcism'. The details are recounted in the book *Possessed* by Thomas Allen. The events recounted here are troubling enough, but in the book and the film they rainbow into hellish Technicolor. The spectacular vomits, the sexual shenanigans involving the young girl, the death of the old archaeologist exorcist played by Max Von Sydow – none of these have any basis in the original chronicle. People in the auditorium would frequently puke and pass out, so the queues, it goes without saying, grew longer. One recalls *Psycho*, and the dire vicarious sufferings of those who had paid but an hour before to get in.

All of the spectacular effects of *The Exorcist* were in fact unnecessary. What terrifies about Satan and the demons is intelligent cunning and damnable determination, not the multi-coloured yawns of the possessed. It is that which makes them uncanny and terrifying, and it is that quality of hellishness which connects them with the goings-on in *From Hell*. This quality of transcendent and merciless intelligence is what intrigues us about infernal agents. In *Jaws*, the Great White shark is endowed with a vengeful intelligence, something no shark has ever been observed actually to possess in nature. This is a shark with a plan; it is a revenger. It is this which connects him up with the demonic intelligence which inhabits the young girl in *The Exorcist*, and this which connects him too with Satan in *Paradise Lost*. A transcendent intellect among the ruins of morality and restraint: that is the one unifying factor in all visions of the terror which the infernal agent can bring.

> **It is not the darkness that terrifies in infernal narratives and images; it is the darkness with the preternatural intelligence present inside it; the ravenous cunning that lurks in the dark.**

IT IS THIS quality of supreme intelligence which has fascinated modern writers: Glen Duncan in *I Lucifer*, Robert Irwin in *Satan Wants Me*, and supremely, Jeremy Leven in *Satan: His Psychotherapy and Cure by the Unfortunate Dr. Kassler, J. S. P. S.* In each of these works, all remarkable in their own way, the devil tends to be astoundingly superior in intellect to all his interlocutors and antagonists. It is not the darkness that terrifies in infernal narratives and images; it is the darkness with the preternatural intelligence present inside it; the ravenous cunning that lurks in the dark. Here we might permit ourselves some prehistoric speculation: that what is incised so ineradicably in our psyches was scored there in a time seemingly before remembrance. When the darkness outside the cave (or, before the mastery of fire, even inside it) contained cunning and ravenous beasts that sought to devour us and ours. In that case, our terror of (and fascination with) 'the powers of darkness' is the vestige of a survival mechanism activated at the beginning of our species history. In the dark lurks the enemy. Its intelligence is different from ours; with him there is no apparent pause between thought and physical enactment; there is no gap where the planning takes place.

Those whom we would predate are predators too, and they have a quickness of reaction and movement which is beyond the ponderous bimanous bipeds we have already started becoming. *The Fall of Satan* is an enactment of how that ferocious beast encountered his come-uppance in his fall into the pit during the *battue*, but we know that there is always another creature where he came from. So the demons still emerge from hell, with bright eyes, and swift manoeuvres. They can still lead us to our doom. We are revisiting the primal scene of our earliest and most terrible dangers. In permitting our early enemies to travel so freely through time and space, we render them preternatural. And we also (it needs to be said) render ourselves less bored. Nothing fascinates more than an intelligence outside the precincts of our species, an intelligence capable of reaching beyond our own. This is the fascination of HAL in Kubrick's *2001*: we might have made him up, but now he can go way beyond us, and not just in the playing of a chess game.

Adrian Leverkühn in Thomas Mann's *Doktor Faustus* signs his infernal pact in order to avoid the repetition and pastiche which appear to be the only option open to the modern artist who has not signed an equivalent treaty with the infernal powers. He is seeking an escape from representational repetition. He is prepared to stake his soul on achieving something new. Baudelaire appears to do the same at the end of *Le Voyage*. Even Freud seemed in need of powers from below to refresh his psychological studies into pertinence. The epigraph to *The Interpretation of Dreams* informs us: *Flectere si nequeo Superos, Acheronta movebo*. If heaven can't be moved, then I'll raise hell instead.

Hell has not been entirely abolished yet.

CHAPTER NOTES

1. The Devil (1977)
   Satan (1981)
   Lucifer (1984)
   Mephistopheles (1986)
   The Prince of Darkness (1988)

2. *London Review of Books*, 9 May, 2013.

12.

The poet and the dictionary

Broken Hierarchies: Poems 1952-2012
Geoffrey Hill
Oxford University Press, 2014| pp 992. | $39.95 £35.00

Visionary Philology: Geoffrey Hill and the Study of Words
Matthew Sperling
Oxford University Press, 2014 | pp. 204. | $99.00 £60.00

For if words are not THINGS, they are LIVING POWERS, by which the things of most importance to mankind are actuated, combined and humanized.
— Samuel Taylor Coleridge

HOW WORD-OBSESSED should a poet be? We can watch George Herbert shaping a lark out of the length of his lines in 'Easter Wings', a form reprised by Geoffrey Hill in *Clavics*. We can see John Donne in 'A Nocturnal upon Saint Lucy's Day' ensuring that 'The whole world's sap is sunk' is the most shrunken line of the stanza in terms of its syllable count, and that 'sap' and 'sunk' utter their monosyllabic desolation through the copula. Gerard Manley Hopkins finds a new way of welding words together, at least in part through his intense scrutiny of Old English lexicology and prosody. For a while it seemed that E. E. Cummings was doing something entirely new, but that was an illusion: he was not so much word-obsessed as typewriter-obsessed. What once seemed new now seems merely novel, and novelty withers swiftly on the vine. Then there was Paul Celan, whose neologisms and portmanteau inventions were shaped out of the most serious obsessions any poet might have. This is news that stays news.

The Shakespeare of the Sonnets was one of the most word-obsessed poets ever to have walked amongst us. When he writes 'Ruin hath taught me thus to ruminate/That time will come and take my love away' we have to look hard to see what he saw and heard in the words. If you take the word *mate* and ram *ruin* through it, you will end up anagrammatically with 'ruminate'. What is expressed is enacted in the diction. What is being said is inseparable from the exact lexis and syntax of its saying.

Geoffrey Hill's poetic career has been mediated through his engagement with the dictionary. And that dictionary is first and foremost the OED. There is no greater dictionary in the world, and its making constitutes one of the great intellectual events of the twentieth century, though it started life in the nineteenth. There had never been anything like this before. Now the language itself has become the documented labyrinth of its own manifold meanings. Now history can be traced uttering itself thus and thus in one mutating word after another. The thought of a poet writing in

English who would not grow excited turning the pages of the OED, or clicking on the electronic version, is so dismal that one wishes such a personage an even smaller readership than modern poets normally manage to acquire.

Hill's verse uses lexicography and philology as heuristic principles.

The anti-self to our word-blind, purblind poet is undoubtedly Geoffrey Hill. His verse uses lexicography and philology as heuristic principles. Where Robert Graves leapt out of the window after Laura Riding (even if he did go down a storey first), one suspects it would require the defenestration of Hill's beloved bound set of the *OED* to elicit any such voluntary *lapsus* from him. The White Goddess, being no better than she should be, might have had a slightly harder time of it, had she been strutting her stuff in Worcestershire. With A. E. Housman to the left of her, and Geoffrey Hill to the right, she would have received some very old-fashioned looks indeed; chilly gazes from fellows not so easily beguiled. And acerbity is a necessary part of our theme. Acerbity is integral to Hill's achievements in both verse and prose. Sentimentality is anathema. There are no flies on this fellow. The constable's son is nothing if not forensic. Every emotion is likely to be treated as the scene of a crime, past, present, or to come.

EVERYONE KNOWS HOW awful William McGonagall is, but it is seldom pointed out why. His rhyming is a low addiction, to which the natural word-order is always sacrificed. He has no ear for cliché, and therefore cliché takes complete command. But there is something else. He is unrelentingly *bien-pensant*. By the time he has finished lamenting the loss of ninety lives in the *Tay Bridge Disaster of 1879*, one is almost hoping for even more hideous fatalities, if only to add some acid piquancy to so much unrelenting gush. It is a relief to turn from such well-meaning palavers to these lines in Beckett's *Malone Dies*: 'Let me say before I go any further that I forgive nobody. I wish them all an atrocious life and then the fires and ice of hell and in the execrable generations to come an honoured name.' Dante, after all, devotes a third of his masterpiece to a close observation of those damned in perpetuity. At one point Virgil feels obliged to rebuke him for his inordinate empathy. To relate so feelingly to those condemned to ceaseless suffering might be seen as a rebuke to the grand order of things; that *cosmos* instituted and maintained by divine power.

How exact can language be? What is the relationship between writing and expressible truth? If one question is rooted at the centre of any serious poetic endeavour, it is surely this. Paul Celan (a figure of considerable importance to Hill) probes the words he is using to such an extent that molecular lexemes break up or re-form. We see this in the wonderful innovation *atemwende*, or breath-turn. If this is playfulness, the game is one of the greatest gravity. And that last word ushers us in to the nature of our problem, which begins in the seventeenth century: the relationship between language, as employed in verse, and language employed in science. Gravity can be expressed in an equation derived by Isaac Newton. It is also, by metaphoric extension, a term denoting how weighty our intellectual seriousness might be deemed to be. And so we have Hill in *Scenes from Comus*:

> Milton meant civil war
> and civil detractions, and the sway of power,
> the pull of power, its *pondus*, its gravity.

In *Leviathan* Hobbes described geometry as the only genuine science, and he praised the fact that there 'men begin at settling the significations of their words'. This is evidently a state of affairs greatly to be desired. Aubrey tells us that Hobbes was forty before he ever peered into Euclid. Then he became obsessed. 'I have heard Mr. Hobbes say that he was wont to draw lines on his thigh and on the sheetes, abed, and also multiply and divide.' What evidently delighted Hobbes about geometry was its lack of what Thomas Sprat in his *History of the Royal Society* called 'this vicious abundance of phrase'. It was a great preoccupation of the time. Could language utter truth without catachresis, deviation, superfluity or decoration? Swift shows us the two extremes adumbrated by language theory: the philosophers in Lagado who carry a bag of objects on their back, so they can indicate the precise item signified without any imprecision of lexis, and the endless metaphoric multiplications and plurabilities to which we are treated in *A Tale of a Tub*. This was the same question Wittgenstein was asking himself in the *Tractatus*, and it is a question Hill's verse never sallies far away from. Take his justly famous 'September Song', and the three middle lines:

> (I have made
> an elegy for myself it
> is true)

The parenthetical aside might be soliloquising. If there is any truth to be had here, it seems to say, it is personal. Goebbels reckoned that the greater the number of fatalities, the further we travelled from tragedy towards statistics, and the less it really meant. A public address might be considerably more suspect, as was Brooke's elegy for the nation — composed before his experience of any actual deaths — in 'The Soldier', and yet we must question this parenthesis too. If Hill has made an elegy for himself, then why publish it? And would its truth be affected either way? The poem does feel 'overheard', and that is part of its distinction. Its tact and recalcitrance achieve precisely the right tone. Anything louder, anything that was more of a broadcast, would feel less sincere, more noisily 'caring'. And if we recall the etymology of 'broadcast' as originally signifying the most promiscuous manner of casting seed, then we could say that Brooke's sonnet was overseeded. And the precision of language here is an aspect of that tact and recalcitrance, which reveal the poetic intelligence at work.

BUT WE MUST ask once more, because it is central to Hill's endeavours, as it was central to Celan's: how precise can language be? How far can it express anything 'that is the case'? Let us use a crude example. Here is a sentence which seems at first sight unproblematical: 'I observe the electron and change its state and position.' As Niels Bohr told us, time after time, we are suspended in language. And so we are, but the suspension here starts to become viscous. Things soon get sticky. Every word of our sentence begs questions that the formulation of the sentence cannot by itself resolve. The *I* that is observing here is not merely the human eye and mind but a vast machinery, a machinery far more complex than that which any amateur scientist could afford to assemble, unless you are rich enough to build your own **CERN**. *Observe* feels passive, unobtrusive, as in 'I observe the moon'. But here the act of observation requires the directing of energy towards the subatomic subject. Observation in this instance is both aggressive and transformative. The definite article that follows is, according to David Bohm, an illicit transfer of categories from the macrocosmic to the microcosmic. We talk of *the* electron as if it were an apple, but Bohm says that the use of nouns here to describe elementary particles is misleading: verbs would be better in indicating the matter at hand, since nominal enclosure misrepresents the fleeting identity.

An electron is in a perpetual state of movement and dynamic relationship. Stop the movement or the relationship and you cease to have that particular electron. The conjunction *and*, given the syntagmatic axis of communication along which syntax inevitably orients itself, implies sequence, chronology, succession. But by the time we arrive at the word *and*, the crucial change has already taken place, because the next word *change* took place at the precise instant of observation, back at the beginning of the sentence. *And* would like to represent itself as an equals sign, but it is altogether too late for that. So the following possessive pronoun *its* is now referring to an electron which is no longer the electron being observed at the beginning of the sentence. It is no longer what or where it was when we got started. If it has jumped from the ground state to an excited state above, then the 'object' to be observed has in effect become a different 'object' through the act of observation; 'it' has changed 'its' state and position. *It* is no longer there. And we invoke Heisenberg to remind ourselves that the knowledge of the particle's velocity and the knowledge of its position are in an inverse relation, one to another. We might also note in passing that the word electron takes us back to the Greek word for amber; that using the word *jump* is a personification which attributes motivation to an elementary particle; that 'ground state' and 'excited state' mingle a topographic model with an emotional one. We are suspended in language, involved in etymology, rhetoric, metaphor, and anthropomorphism. So how precise is it possible to be here? How exact can language ever be? Grammar here amounts to fallenness. This is Hill's line anyway, and he argues in *The Orchards of Syon* that the angels are free from grammar:

> I mean they're beyond grammar that reminds
> us of our fall, and of hanging out there.

Well, angelological linguistics, prelapsarian or not, can be a tricky business, as even Hill would presumably concede. Studying the Enochian language decoded by Dr John Dee, after the nightly skrying of Edward Kelley, does not necessarily get us much further.

Our short seemingly unproblematical sentence has turned out to be full of actually unendurable problems. Were things ever thus? Owen Barfield reckoned that our primal language was a vast porosity of borders, a metaphoric prairie in which we were free to roam. It is a beguiling notion, but one that is impossible to prove. In any case, I would like to argue that it is Hill's awareness of this density of difficulty in language as both expression and representation that makes him such a formidable literary figure. His understanding that, to use Yeats's phrase, 'difficulty is our plough' makes him not merely exemplary but exhilarating too, for those prepared to make the textual journey, which presumably includes any who have read thus far in this review. We must make everything as simple as possible, Einstein remarked — but no simpler. Hill remarks in one of his essays how he constantly registers 'how recalcitrant, how obstructive, this material is.' The material is language and the more the density of this medium is felt as a specific gravity, the more likely the writer is to exhibit the wished-for intelligence in his writing. The more effortless the movement through language, the stupider the finished text is likely to be. Such stupidity can be effortlessly disguised by irony, snug in its own oil-slick of surface cleverness.

A POEM FROM Hill's first book hinges on a single word. The word is *pinnacle*, and Hill has detected in it a Janus face of double possibility, since it can refer both to natural forms and architecture.

Merlin

I will consider the outnumbering dead:
For they are the husks of what was rich seed.
Now, should they come together to be fed,
They would outstrip the locusts' covering tide.

Arthur, Elaine, Mordred; they are all gone
Among the raftered galleries of bone.
By the long barrows of Logres they are made one,
And over their city stands the pinnacled corn.

Human beings and seeds; all flesh is grass. More of the dead figures stand shadily behind us than the living ones who currently stand beside us. And once more we observe that lack of sentimentality (not sentiment) which characterises all his work, with the possible exception of some of the poems in *Tenebrae*. But the clinching word, the word which locks the separate perceptions together, is *pinnacled*. It is a curious word, bringing together in its original Latin the *wing* and the *peak*.

Hill is an inquisitor, the etymological researcher into the besmirched history of lexis.

'Philosophy is a battle against the bewitchment of our intelligence by means of language.' So wrote Wittgenstein, and Hill seems to be saying something remarkably similar, particularly in the later work. Words and phrases are interrogated; their precise meaning demanded of them. The poet here is an inquisitor, the etymological researcher into the besmirched history of lexis. And right at the beginning of his career as a poet, the corn here is pinnacled, as was Camelot. And both fall into the earth, among the raftered galleries of bone. Jesus declared that the temple, to whose pinnacle Satan so breezily lifted him, would be pulled down but would rise again. So the pinnacled temple was both the grand edifice in Jerusalem, and also his body. And Merlin is of course an intelligence detachable from the social and historical circumstances in which we usually know him; he is transcendent. He is also, one might note, unsentimental. Things are thus and thus. It is the poet's duty to transcribe them accurately, and as Hill writes elsewhere: 'In a successful poem a particular word may instantaneously perform what it desiderates.' Such a word is *pinnacled* in 'Merlin'.

Wittgenstein believed that the best philosophy could hope for was accurate description, and the movement in science known in the 1890s as 'descriptionism' espoused the same notion. All science could do, claimed its main advocates Ernst Mach and Karl Pearson, was to describe the phenomena, with the most finely calibrated descriptive technique. Nothing could ever be explained. The only answer to the question, 'Why is it thus?' is, in effect, 'Because it is.' Newton, we might recall, insisted *'Hypotheses non fingo'* – I don't hypothesise. I try to describe the way things are; it wasn't me who brought all this about, after all.

NOW THIS IS the intellectual world into which the intellectually alert poet finds himself thrown. What is to be done? There is no escape to be had from thinking, despite Yeats in his wilder moments sometimes thinking there might be. In some of his poems Hill the lexicographer is indistinguishable from Hill the poet. The words of our language carry our history, like tiny freighted vehicles, each one revealing or hiding its own monographic narrative. So we have this, for example:

Strophe after strophe
ever more catastrophic. Did I say
strophe? I meant salvo, sorry.

Here the jostling lexemes of the verse are effectively involved in a punch-up.

How can we put this? Every poem is a figure, and the ground against which that figure stands is the contemporary usage of the language. Poetry insists that its figure is to be distinguished from its immediate linguistic environs, its surrounding ground, by certain defining characteristics: lines shaped by the eye and ear of the poet, not merely by the typographic conventions of the printed page. Lineation is a species of punctuation, and T. S. Eliot insisted that, whatever else poetry is, it is always a form of punctuation. We see this in Eliot's own practice at its best:

> All this was a long time ago, I remember,
> And I would do it again, but set down
> This set down
> This: were we led all that way for
> Birth or Death?

No poetry was ever better punctuated than this, where the lineation has rid itself of all supernumerary marks. The reading eye is addressed directly and with modernist economy. Here the figure clearly distinguishes itself from the ground. The elliptical compression of poetry consumes the vernacular energy that swirls around it, only to re-issue that language as a defamiliarized usage, making it new, figuring such new-fangledness as shaped verse. And an inevitable part of that underlying lexical ground is cliché, or something that is slightly different: iterative vernacular vigour.

Between rancour and cliché the serious writer must somehow find his way. Is there another major figure in the arts so devoted to the use and demolition of cliché as Hill, unless it be Bob Dylan? The latter says of the woman in 'Tangled Up In Blue' that 'I helped her out of a jam, I guess/But I used a little too much force.' And out of the coffin of the cliché steps a meaning, as if night had settled once more on Count Dracula's domicile. Both Dylan and Hill hack away at the ossified rock of cliché, confident there must still be a redeeming fossil in there somewhere. There always is. Both these artists understand in their different forms that cliché is unavoidable; it is implicit in the medium. It is no good closing your eyes and looking pained. Instead then, hunt for the perception that got the cliché going in the first place, so that you might re-translate it into present usage. Make it new, antique or exhausted as it may seem. Some irony may be needed, for a little added piquancy, but never imagine irony gets you off the hook. And mirrors are useful for turning things around. We did our first learning, it seems, through mirror neurons. We learn how to write through parody and pastiche. Some of the finest religious poetry is by way of sacred parody, in which the Almighty is addressed as the beloved. With all the attendant problems such an address implies.

AND SO HILL has Saint Sebastian 'catching his death'. Here the cliché stumbles over itself, and is astonished to discover how much power it appears to have retained. In the more recent 'Ars', a memorial poem for Ken Smith, Hill writes: 'Not everything's a joke, but we've been had.' Can one really call this cliché? The vernacular reiterates itself, certainly, but the repetition should not be called cliché unless it has lost all its original natural vigour. Here its taughtness and tartness feel precisely right. In the same way, Dylan in a recent song sang 'Something's out of whack.' If the available phrase is the most potent one, then use it. And Hill is determined to stay tuned in to the language around him. He recently gave us *tittagram* and *recite-a-thon*, neither of which has yet made it into the *OED*. The word *demobbed* had only just made it into the *OED* two years before when it found itself included in *The Waste Land*, as a result of Pound's ear for the language of the street, rather than Eliot's. It was E.P.'s suggested addition on the typescript.

Hill regards postmodernism as a collapse of the necessary resistance of the artist, where modernism in its exemplary forms represented that resistance incarnate.

The poet must be attuned to the language uttered around him, but he must not succumb to its mores. A key word in Hill's intellectual armoury is *resistance*. Hill regards postmodernism as a collapse of the necessary resistance of the artist, where modernism in its exemplary forms represented that resistance incarnate. In the breezy ironic whimsicalities of so much postmodernism, Hill sees a craven populism dressed up in the gladrags of cultural fashion. Modernism was hard; it never forgot that 'difficulty is our plough'. The greatest tribute to the common reader, according to Hill, is the offer of serious difficulty encountered on the page. Not the snapshot slickness embodied in words like *tittagram* and *recite-a-thon*. So what is the difference between a modernist approach to the present and the past, and its postmodernist counterparts?

The modernists encountered the past, not in order to recapitulate it, but to make it new. This meant that they were actually more obsessed with the past than their predecessors. They were wrestling more agonistically with what had been inherited and had to be transmuted. *The Cantos* begins with Homer, *The Waste Land* begins with Chaucer. But the central modernist perception is this: present language and our existing forms are only possible because of our prior language and prior forms, but we live now, with this language in its current state of use. Simple reiteration or pastiche will not do. So the present language of our verse must demonstrate its awareness of the tradition, but it must extend it at the same time.

IF THERE IS a central allusion in *Mercian Hymns* it is not so much historic as stylistic. We could trace it back to Pound's *Homage to Sextus Propertius*. There Pound went in for a species of braiding, interleaving the linguistic usage of the present with the *materia* of the distant past. The effect is a defamiliarization, a frisson as we register the dissonance between then and now, while still focussing with all due attention on then. The obverse of present usage is backed by the reverse of historic allusion, but there is only ever one coin, and that is the text being created. It is a technique of anti-pastiche, a refusal of the historicist fancy-dress party that any 'historical work' can too easily become. Pound's central understanding was that the work, whatever its subject, must be contemporary; the language must be heard to be living now. Even in his 'The Seafarer', which is the nearest he ever got to straight transcription, he somehow finds an echo of the pulse of a modern rhythm in the old lines.

Now when Basil Bunting had a copy of Pound's *Sextus* put into his hands in 1919 by Nina Hamnett, he could see immediately that nothing would ever be the same again. And it never was. First, he became Villon transported to a contemporary French prison cell. And then he was writing *Briggflatts*, constantly holding before himself the braiding of letters and creatures in the illuminated pages of the Lindisfarne Gospels, and on every page of his own poem he braided present usage, present vocabulary and authentic contemporaray rhythm with the historical data of an Anglo-Saxon chronicle. Thus did he make it new, as Pound had commanded. And Hill achieves a similar effect in the *Hymns*. His braiding of Offa's ceremonial court and the doings of contemporary car salesmen from the Midlands forms its own interleaving pattern. But it never evaporates into postmodernist whimsy, which all too often pleads irony as alibi. Irony as a substitute for all other modes or beliefs. Irony as guarantor of an acceptable shallowness; the universal corrosive.

THERE ALSO LURKS behind Pound's *Sextus* the loopiness of the crib, and the kind of language it can elicit from the unwary.

Housman had been on to this before in his 'Fragment of a Greek Tragedy':

> *Chorus:* O suitably attired in leather boots
> Head of a traveller, wherefore seeking whom
> Whence by what way how purposed art thou come
> To this well-nightingaled vicinity?
> My object in inquiring is to know.
> But if you happen to be deaf and dumb
> And do not understand a word I say,
> Nod with your hand to signify as much.

Yes, quite. Which is another way of saying, there is no such thing as a literal translation, because different languages have different ways of functioning. You can transliterate a word, but if you do it with sentences, they will rapidly become ridiculous.

So what is it that the modern poem, with the seriousness of the modernist achievement behind it, seeks to achieve? Perhaps one of the best ways to think about what a poem does is to use Gerard Manley Hopkin's word *inscape*. Inscape is spiritual constellation. It can only be achieved by the vigorous and unsentimental ordering of form within the medium of materials to be disposed. In a poem those materials are words, syntax, rhythm and rhyme. Though we might also bear in mind Pound's three poetic functions in *The ABC of Reading*: logopeia, phanopeia and melopeia. Or lexis, imagery and musical effect.

WHAT HOPKINS MEANS by inscape can be related to what Wittgenstein meant when he said that anything could represent anything else as long as they held between them a shared form. A vinyl record can represent a symphony if the variegated depth of its grooves corresponds to the set of sounds that constitutes the opus; the same is true of a musical score, or of the diagrammatic relationship between a map and a landscape. And the same was true, as far as Wittgenstein was concerned, whenever a sentence exhibited its structural and logical cohesion satisfactorily. It thereby uttered a truth about the nature of things. It showed the nature of 'everything that is the case'. Its logical form was an expression of the way in which things are disposed thus and thus: the standard model of possible meanings.

The nature of the form here is all-important. For example, Hopkins criticised a painting by Holman Hunt thus: 'It has no inscape of composition whatsoever.' Here the 'realism' of the picture had become what Brancusi marvellously called 'a confusion of familiarities'. Realism as a technique is a surface affair; it reproduces superficial detail; it merely conveys the actual, as a conveyor-belt transports the fashioned items from here to there. What is needed is to convert the actual into the real, or to so cleanse those Blakean doors of perception that the real shines through the actual, illuminating form from within. Then we have inscape: the necessary constellation of perceptions.

This confusion of a certain type of realism with inscape is what elicited Paul Celan's lifelong rage against the mode of writing Northrop Frye once called 'the low-mimetic'. Hill has carried on the railing. The notion that the accumulation of detail (usually, the more sordid the better) somehow conveys the nature of reality is one of the more fatuous notions of our time, together with the related fatuity that art is indistinguishable from self-expression. The reason Walter Benjamin was so fascinated by Surrealism was that he believed its new constellation was truer, in a sense more realistic, than other modes of art on offer at the time. The new constellation had to include the content of dreams, those commando raids on the city's daily order instigated by the units of the Unconscious during the night. To exclude such data in the age of Freud was to be unrealistic about artistic requirements. Realism of the old sort could look like an intellectually unsatisfactory exclusivism; a hollow reiteration. Or pastiche by another name. Adrian Leverkühn in Thomas Mann's *Doktor Faustus* is prepared to sell his soul to the devil in order to avoid the most dreaded cultural fate: the ceaseless repetition of existing contents in existing forms. The notion that art is no more than a pantomime of repeat performances.

SO WHAT ARE we to write about, if difficulty is our plough? In 1853, Matthew Arnold wrote the Introduction to his *Collected Poems*. He explained there why he had left out *Empedocles on Etna*, published the previous year. He had done so because he had come to feel that the suffering in that dramatic poem found 'no vent in action'. In 1936, when Yeats edited *The Oxford Book of Modern Verse*, he alluded to Arnold's Introduction, in explaining why he had omitted the poetry of Wilfred Owen – then as now a great favourite – on the grounds that too much of it was concerned with passive suffering. It would doubtless have come as news to many members of the British Expeditionary Force that their prime experience on the Western Front had been one of passive suffering, but it is a pity that Arnold's Introduction has now become notorious only for this particular exclusion. Arnold makes some very telling comparisons between the poetry of his time and that of the ancients. He finds that the undoubted linguistic genius of, for example, Keats, cannot compensate for certain fundamental flaws of dramatic presentation. He argues that when Keats writes 'Isabella', his dramatization of that tale is not a patch on the original in Boccaccio. He is arguing, in effect, that the writing of his contemporaries tends to forfeit the historical in favour of the emotional; the dramatic in favour of the pyrotechnics of linguistic inventiveness; characterisation in favour of the shallowly spectacular. All he had to say then is surely worth repeating now.

> **Hill has refused to be distracted by the trivialities of our age, and the low-mimetic prattle that so frequently accompanies them.**

The modernists in effect heeded Arnold's injunctions, though he was one of the last authorities they would usually have invoked. *The Waste Land* is a public poem, in which Tiresias has forgotten nothing of antiquity. *The Cantos* is structured by ancient patternings. And so is *Ulysses*, where Homeric characterizations and plots find their corollary in the goings-on of contemporary Dublin. They offer a form. Plot is crucial to them all. And plot means subject-matter, just as subject-matter means choice of subject. Hill has been criticised by his detractors for being altogether too grand. What this means, in effect, is that he chooses big themes, and harps upon them. What the detractors disparage is precisely what his supporters praise. He has refused to be distracted by the trivialities of our age, and the low-mimetic prattle that so frequently accompanies them. All those piss-takes; so many cleverdick routines. How we chortled. The tittagram would not be long in coming. Soon enough we might find ourselves forming a chorus in the recite-a-thon. Not everything's a joke though, is it? Hill insists on that. And we've certainly been had. Write about what you know, the writing students are enjoined.

And thus is the whole point of the endeavour instantly lost. Writing is a cognitive activity: it is a way of getting to know, not a mere mechanical exposition of what we found out earlier, and shall now copy out in time for the workshop.

In his passionate and haunting poem 'In Memoriam: Gillian Rose', Hill demonstrates how personal one can be in verse without needing to go into the 'confessional mode'. In one sense the poem is a compressed review of three books by Rose, who died young, but achieved much nonetheless. The books are: *Mourning Becomes the Law*, *Love's Work* and *Paradiso*. He is returning upon her through her books, but then she returned upon herself through her books too, so the circularity is a blessed one. The first of these titles exhibits the kind of unapologetic difficulty Hill applauds. The second two constitute a self-elegy. That's a selfie in words with no protective whimsy to act as exoskeleton. 'Love's work' Hill finds 'a bleak ontology', but he goes on to say at the finishing-line: 'it may be all we have'.

IN 1989, THE second complete edition of the *OED* was published in twenty volumes. Hill was sent his reviewer's copies from the Clarendon Press, via the *TLS*, and proceeded instantly to complain. The complaint was fascinating and entirely characteristic. But let us wind back a little.

The first fascicle of this vast enterprise (A-ANT) was published in 1884, and the first completed edition appeared in 1928, to be followed in 1933 by the Supplement. A further four-volume supplement was published in its entirety in 1986, under the editorship of Robert Burchfield. And then in 1989 came the second complete edition. Since then the whole text has been digitalised and put online. The lengthy business effectively started back in

1857 with a paper delivered to the Philological Society entitled 'On Some Deficiencies in Our English Dictionaries'. That had been given by Richard Chevenix Trench, one-time Dean of Westminster and subsequently Archbishop of Dublin. Trench, who receives a whole chapter to himself in Matthew Sperling's excellent *Visionary Philology: Geoffrey Hill and the Study of Words*, was a popular lexicographer. He published books with titles such as *On the Study of Words*, which are as readable and engaging today as they were when first published. His fastidious lexical hunting and parsing makes him a progenitor of that word-hungry poet, Geoffrey Hill. To garble, he points out in his *A Select Glossary of English Words Used Formerly in Senses Different from Their Present*, was once 'to sift or cleanse corn from any dust or rubbish which may have become mingled with it.' It was, in other words, to separate the good from the bad. How times change, not always for the better. Our garbling has become garbled.

Sperling's book is a brilliant, sprightly text, which is a delight to read. It is an account of the entanglement of Hill's work with etymology and lexicography; so entangled are they, so dialectically intertwined, that I would say they are inextricable. Trench cheerfully swiped Emerson's phrase 'fossil poetry' to describe the way history encodes and engrafts itself on to and into language. Hill is always aware of the fossilized meanings which etymology uncovers. One can only do such work with the aid of the dictionary, of course. No one writer, however vastly learned, could manage all this work for himself. This is why Hill ended his OED review with a magisterial flourish: 'Most of what one wants to know, including much that it hurts to know, about the English language is held within these twenty volumes. To brood over them and in them is to be finally persuaded that sematology is a theological dimension: the use of language is inseparable from the "terrible aboriginal calamity" in which, according to Newman, the human race is implicated.' That aboriginal calamity is another name for Original Sin. And *sematology* was a word much used by the early OED editors. We would now normally say semiotics, if with a particular linguistic bent.

And so in a sense Sperling's book brings us back to where we started. The linguistic turn at the start of the twentieth century was an acknowledgment of the inescapability of language. The most witless error possible is to imagine that language simply translates our thought into constellations of linguistic signs. The point is that we can only think in the first place through these signs. We are shaped by them as much as we come to shape them in our turn. We are named before we can speak. We find our being and identity through language. Language is as much the medium through which our thought has life, as air is the medium through which we breathe. The dictionary is not merely there to explain unknown words; it is there to make possible the exploration of the illimitable linguistic dimension we call our thought. It is a vast field of battles fought and negotiations concluded. Hill would immediately point out how the word negotiate, in its Latin origins, involves us etymologically in the cancellation of leisure. In one sense the OED is, collectively speaking, our greatest work.

So what was the specific nature of Hill's grouse about the *OED*, after he had unpacked his free copies? He was unhappy about the editors' gloss on the word *disremembering*. He felt that Gerard Manley Hopkins' usage, in his poem 'Spelt from Sybil's Leaves', offered a widening of the meaning which had not been supplied in the dictionary's pages. In the Hopkins poem, the meaning is not a casual forgetting, but the dismemberment of memory itself. And that makes a difference.

Cantankerous, contrary, never less than passionate. In a poetic age profiled by postmodernist tricksters and oleaginous courtiers heading for their gongs, we are certainly lucky to have him.

13.

Textuality: Ephesus and Patmos

1. THE FOURTH GOSPEL.

WHAT IS A text? If it is 'a canonic text', then a certain amount of thought must have gone into the matter. The OED says the word *canonical* means that something is 'authoritative; orthodox; standard'. And it says that the canon itself is 'the list of books of the Bible accepted by the Christian Church as genuine and inspired'. So far, so straightforward then. But not for long. Should we turn to Tyndale's version of the Gospels we will find some highly charged words being used. Why? The ghost of Tyndale's text lurks behind half of the words of the King James Bible, though many had to be modified in order to assuage the powers that be (one of the phrases Tyndale had recently invented) in the subsequent editions that were to use so many of his words, without ever mentioning his name. His memory was simply too troublesome.

Tyndale was trying to get back to the Greek original, so as to avoid any unwanted textual accoutrements which had sprouted up through the centuries; the way the wishes of man have so often imposed themselves on revelation. What did the biblical words mean, before the Church had started to build its mighty edifice of interpretation upon them? What was Jesus actually trying to say fifteen hundred years before? If we could reverse the allegorical thrust of so much of the tradition, pull the text back from emblems and analogies, and thereby arrive at the original sense, as an actual account of actual events, we might once more find that the truth can set you free. He was eloquent on the subject: 'I call God to record, against the day we shall appear before our Lord Jesus, to give a reckoning of our doings, that I never altered one syllable of God's word against my conscience, nor would this day, if all that is in the earth, whether it be pleasure, honour or riches, might be given me.' This was dangerous ground in 1525, since translating the Bible into English without authorization was illegal. Tyndale had to get out of England to do it. And his translation pressed his own case, the case of an impassioned reformer. Instead of *charity*, he used the word *love*; instead of *priest*, he wrote *elder*; instead of *church*, he said *congregation*. This was non-ecclesiastical language. Some thought it anti-ecclesiastical. It could cost you your life. It cost Tyndale his.

No word is ever straightforwardly translatable into another language. All translations are interpretations and conversions. *Bread*, *pain*, and *Brot* might all be recorded as synonymous, but each carries a freight of tradition, association and cultural expectation. Should I now add that this bread is of heaven, then the terms *paradis* or

Himmel are enough to project us into another linguistic universe entirely. Tyndale's use of *congregation* instead of *church* was strikingly polemical.

Tyndale gives us, as do most of our familiar modern English versions, the *Pericope Adulterae*, the passage in which Jesus is confronted with the woman taken in adultery and invited to condemn her. The earliest Greek texts of the Gospel do not contain this passage, and it has been speculated that it was a later interpolation, with a specific purpose: to show that Jesus was fully literate, that he could write as well as read.[1] This is the only occasion in any of the Gospels when Jesus does write, and his own words are immediately obliterated, since they are written in dust, as Keats feared his own name might be 'writ in water'. Why did Jesus leave us no text from his own hand? He is constantly quoting from Hebrew scripture; he appears to be honeycombed with it. But never does he sit down for an hour with a stylus, in order to make clear the fundamentals of his mission and his teaching to his followers. This is a curiosity worthy of note, since he must surely have anticipated how soon the quarrels might get started after his death, and they have of course never ceased since. The curiosity is one that has recently taken on a further edge: the distinguished scholar Geza Vermes insisted that the word *naggar*, the Aramaic word for carpenter, also meant a shaper of words, an interpreter of texts, and that this word employed in the Palestinian Judaism of Jesus's day would have been more likely to have had the second, metaphoric meaning, than the first and literal one – in the same way that a 'mechanic' in a poker game is nowadays a cheat. In other words, Jeshua the carpenter, son of Joseph the carpenter from Nazareth, should really be (if everything is hinging here on the word *naggar*) Jesus the interpreter of the sacred text, son of Joseph the rabbinic scholar. This feels very similar to Tyndale using *congregation* instead of *church*, or *elder* rather than *priest*: a whole world of meaning hinges upon a single word in a text. And a great many paintings of Jesus as a boy in the carpenter's shop would be shown to have dubious linguistic foundations.

THERE IS A beautiful watercolour by William Blake that shows Jesus writing in the dust after the accusers have presented him with the woman taken in adultery. The text is unique to John. He is writing something with great concentration, and the accusers are now leaving. This is the only occasion when Jesus's body is presented by Blake as a figure of closure, like his portrayal of Newton and Nebuchadnezzar. And for once there is hardly any light emitting from the Saviour's body – another oddity in Blake's iconography. Given Blake's antinomian reading of the Bible, there could be a reason for this: it is the only occasion in all the accounts when Jesus is writing, and what he is writing is the letter of the Law which, according to Blake, his own mission is designed to cancel. There was a strong tradition in the Byzantine tradition, still popular in parts of Russia today, that says that what Jesus wrote in the dust were the sins of the accusers. As they read them they realised that, since they were evidently not without sin themselves, then they could not throw the first stone either. And that is why, uniquely in this pericope, they are said to leave 'one by one'.

Even if he had had any doubts about the pericope's authenticity, this little tale surely fitted Tyndale's purposes admirably. He was on the side of the humble interpreters of the Bible's teaching, against those who thought themselves supreme authorities. Hence his famous statement: 'If God spare my life, ere many years I will cause a boy that driveth the plough shall know more of the scripture than thou dost.' This was addressed to a theological opponent, one said to be learned, whose position in society was somewhat grander than following a plough. We all have the right to midrash; to that questioning of the original scripture, as long as it is driven by a fierce will to get to the truth. Pushed on by the ploughman's shoulder.

What to leave in, and what to take out? And which words to use, so as to convey the authenticity of the original text most forcefully? That is effectively the story of the canon itself, and of every text within it. Should the Book of Revelation have been banished from the lectionary, as it is in the Eastern Orthodox tradition? Luther thought so for a long time, before ultimately changing his mind. Many were troubled by it at the time of its inclusion, and its riddles and ambiguities are probably the cause of as much mischief now as any other book of the Bible. Numerologists delight in its formulae for calculating the final calamity. For centuries it was generally held that it had come from the same hand as the Fourth Gospel. Few would argue this now, so different are the mental worlds conveyed by the two texts; so radically at variance is the language employed. But then few would now argue that the Fourth Gospel was actually written by the Beloved Disciple, the son of Zebedee portrayed in it, though others might still want to argue that much of it can trace a route that goes back ultimately to him. Maybe in a community in Ephesus, or maybe one in Antioch, or Alexandria. The Golan Heights have been mooted, as another possibility. We have become very textual regarding these texts. Very stylistic. Fastidiously historical. Troubled as to how much we can actually know. And then of course there is the question of form.

> **What to leave in, and what to take out? That is effectively the story of the canon itself, and of every text within it.**

It was His finger which inscribed the stone tablets Moses brought down from the mountain, His finger that wrote on the wall at Belshazzar's Feast: you have been weighed in the scales and found wanting. Belshazzar died later that night, they say. And it might have been this finger that Blake is portraying in action for the last time, when Jesus writes in the dust. This is the last enunciation of 'Thou shalt not' by one who is divine. And Jesus only propounds the law in order to abrogate it. It is written not on a scroll or codex, but in the dust where its traces might be kicked over. 'Have none of them condemned thee?' 'No Lord.' 'Then neither do I condemn thee.' The law is abrogated through the action of divine mercy. You have been freed from the letter of the text, so that you might exult at last in its spirit.

NOW BLAKE IS, in Harold Bloom's sense, one of the strongest readers in the language. And he is never a stronger reader than when he is disinterring the Bible from its burial in social convention, by those he insists are its misinterpreters. In *The Everlasting Gospel* he makes it clear that the finger which wrote its commands in the sky is now gone for ever, and that therefore there is no one left to throw the first stone. In other words, Jesus can be seen propounding the law for the last time when he writes in the dust. And he is making it plain that, kicked over in the dust down there, is precisely where the letter of the law belongs. Blake's watercolour of the woman taken in adultery is in effect a visual midrash.

It was during the nineteenth century that we adopted the notion of uniformitarianism in regard to geology. This insisted that the same laws applied back in the mists of time as apply now. That we are not to explain our origins through catastrophism, but by assuming that the same processes of erosion took place yesterday as take place today. The various liberal modifications of Christology during the same century were doing something parallel. There was a mythic accretion around the gospel narratives that had to be accepted as what it was: legendary matter. And then at the heart of this we might find the true figure of Jesus, lurking inside the tangled outgrowths of the very texts he had generated by the power of his presence, the potency of his words. Matthew Arnold was in no doubt that all the accounts of the miracles in the gospel were neither more nor less than a sop by the early church to the credulous and uneducated. They would therefore appear incredible (and rightly so) to any educated modern person.

So how then did we ever get the account of the miraculous birth of Jesus? Well, it's never mentioned by Paul, the earliest of the texts we might confidently verify, and no mention is made of it in Mark either. As for John, he is going back much further in his opening; he is going back before time itself. How come? One answer is that the accounts of the birth in Matthew and Luke answered an early accusation against the early followers of Jesus, namely that the man they acclaimed the Messiah had had an irregular birth; that he was in fact a bastard. This was William Blake's line precisely, except that he regarded it as an antinomian qualification; an embryonic certificate of authenticity for the mission ahead. Matthew and Luke effectively say, in reply to the accusation: You are quite right, and yes, his birth was most unusual. Not through any impropriety, however, but as a result of divine intervention. So then a word in the text of Isaiah, *alma*, with no hint of virginity in it, transmutes into a prophecy of *parthenos*, the virgin who gives birth to the Lord. Thus does the translation of one word in a text radically transmute the whole narrative into a different world of meaning. (Something similar happens as Messiah becomes Christ; we shift culturally from one intellectual universe to another, without any announcement of the fact.)

In the meantime, that journey to Bethlehem in Luke — for a census unmentioned elsewhere in the historical record — permits another rebuttal: how could the Messiah conceivably have come from Galilee? Nowhere in scripture is this predicted or even allowed. So, the child we are presented with is now actually born in David's city, and then that problem has been solved by the latest text too. Here the elaboration of the text takes the form of a series of answers to questions now largely forgotten, like rhyming slang that has jettisoned the word with which it once rhymed. But we must ask ourselves a demanding textual question: how come there is no mention of this extraordinary birth in Mark, the earliest of the synoptic gospels, and how come Paul never makes any mention of the fact either? Surely he, of all people, would have made something of the fact that Jesus had been born without the necessity of the normally required human agency? Between Mark and Paul the elaborations have begun, the answers constructed, the credulous start to be fed their fables and fantastications. And now? What are we to do here in our interpretative work? Away with catastrophism, we have insisted; let's get on with the uniformitarian interpretation. If it could happen yesterday, then it can happen today. Otherwise, we're away with the fairies. Blake had no difficulties with this at all. He reckoned that Joseph and Mary did clear off out of Galilee for the birth, in order to hide the fact that the child was not Joseph's, but then nor was it God's either, at least not in Luke or Matthew's sense, even if it was indeed God's in another sense. The Son of Man was, Blake insists, the divine in human form, but still you cannot break the laws of nature, and neither could he. Otherwise they would not be laws, now would they? The texts of existence cannot be so casually rewritten.

It is possible to think of the infancy narratives in both Luke and Matthew as a form of midrash. In the Jewish tradition, midrash represents a return upon ancient texts. The old text is asked questions it could not have asked itself, and comes up with answers it was not originally obligated to provide. Midrash breaks into the past, and fractures what might otherwise be a hermetically sealed text. Discovering difficulties and gaps which the afterlife of reading has revealed, a later consciousness intrudes and prompts the text (in a synchronous manoeuvre) to further reflections upon aspects of its meaning. It opens past scripture up to the future. The text, it transpires, was richer than anyone had previously thought.

Midrash connects the present of the reader with an historic text....[and] opens up a text to the unlimited possibilities of temporality.

This is what midrash does: it connects the present of the reader with an historic text. It permits the ancient text to ask and answer questions not available to it at the time of its own composition; to put things to itself, as it were, posthumously. In doing this it insists on a text's versatility; its ability to reach out from the point of its composition in the past to the further requirements unfolding in the present. Arthur Eddington used to say that we live in four dimensions. In the first three we have remarkably little extension, but in the fourth, the temporal one, we can travel through a vast territory. Midrash opens up a text to the unlimited possibilities of temporality. And temporality here is inseparable from interpretative thought.

Blake used antinomian imagery all his life. One of his iconographic pairs was the prolific and the devourer. The one generates; the other consumes. It would be hard to think of a more vivid exemplification of this dialectic opposition than the year 1526, as William Tyndale printed copy after copy of his New Testament in English, and the Bishop of London, Tunstall, immediately seized them and had them burnt at St Paul's Cross. Then the Bishop's agents started to cross the Channel and bought the New Testaments on the continent, fresh from the presses, and burned them there instead. The money from these sales immediately financed further revisions, translations and publications. Thus did the devourer prompt the prolific to generate all the more prolifically.

And the same imagery can be seen in Blake's portrayal of the *Woman Taken in Adultery*. She might have sinned but as Jesus says elsewhere, she is forgiven because she has loved much. She is prolific in her affections. The devourers are no more than agents of the Law, the accusers; the word diabolus, from which we derive our word devil, means an accuser. Another tradition holds that what Jesus wrote in the dust was simply their names. And here the scriptural text might allude to its textual foretime: the Book of Jeremiah, where those whose names are written in heaven are saved, while those whose names are written in the earth are lost. Separated from the prolific, the devourer finally devours himself.

SO WHAT ARE the facts about Jesus? William Blake's facts are obviously different from Bishop Tunstall's, but then Tyndale's were different from Tunstall's too, as they were different from those of Thomas More. The facts here are inseparable from the texts in which they are generated and embedded, and that means we must understand the nature of the text if we are ever to try to understand what it is the text communicates; what type of actuality it offers us. When Bishop Ussher used Biblical genealogies to calculate the beginning of the cosmos in 4004 BCE, he was misunderstanding the nature of the text before him. You should not extrapolate scientific chronologies from Hebrew religious poetry. Philip Henry Gosse constructed a similar problem for himself in *Omphalos* in 1857. He was too good a scientist not to acknowledge the reality of the fossils then being unearthed and analysed. But he was too literal a devotee of the word of the Bible to relinquish the account of creation in Genesis. So, he propounded his theory. The fossils are in the earth because God made them, as fossils, and put them there. So as to provide a past for the present to find its footing on. No present, after all, can exist without a past to give meaning to it. The logic here, as Borges argued, is impeccable. The intellectual results catastrophic. He called the process *prochronism*.

A more convincing manoeuvre was enacted when Jewish scholars argued that the findings of modern physics were compatible with the account of creation in Genesis, because of a flexibility in the word *yom*, or day. This does not have to specify a twenty-four hour period, they said, because the sun and moon don't actually appear until after day three. So what orbits would be doing the measuring here? Not those, anyway. This flexibility permits billions of years to cram themselves into those six days of creation in the opening book of the Bible. And God does not even need to fashion fossils. Merely to note to himself (with satisfaction, presumably) the immense flexibility of the word *yom*.

In his brilliant story, 'Proofs of Holy Writ', Rudyard Kipling has Ben Jonson sitting in Shakespeare's garden in 1611. A rider delivers some proofs for revising. The proofs turn out to be proofs of the King James Bible, which Shakespeare has been involved in revising, if not translating. The two playwrights argue about the wording of some lines in Isaiah. How the English version needs to express itself; how the Englishing must proceed according to its own linguistic logic. It is a clever story because Kipling conveys so vividly how finding the right English words and cadences is a matter for the educated ear of the writer; how there is no straightforward and indisputable way of translating any text. The host language insists on its own identity, making its own demands upon writer and reader.

And what a difference one word can make. When Tyndale uses *congregation* to translate *ekklesia*, even though Erasmus had done it before him, he is courting extreme danger. But then in using words the way he did, Jesus courted extreme danger too. They were both of them to be put to death by lawful authorities. One of Tyndale's distinctions is his fondness for rough words, since rough words might better convey rough realities. In chapter five of his Gospel of John he describes the Pool of Bethesda as being close by a *slaughterhouse*. He explains in a marginal gloss that the Greek says 'sheep house', but that it is describing a place where beasts were killed, so his word is the more truthful. By the time the King James version was busily plagiarising Tyndale, his usage here was found too uncouth, and replaced with the word *market*, simultaneously more dainty and less exact. *Abattoir* would come along in the nineteenth century to help a lot of delicate sensibilities with its lexical displacement. The whole thing sounds altogether less bloody in French.

AND THE WORD *slaughterhouse* provides an unexpected angle from which to look at a text and its relation to truth. In 1969, Kurt Vonnegut published his novel *Slaughterhouse-Five*. The title was provided by the large underground meat chamber in which he was incarcerated as a prisoner-of-war in 1945, while Dresden was being firebombed by the Allies. Because he was down there, he survived. Had he been up in the streets, he would have been incinerated, along with so many others. How many, though? The figure Vonnegut gives in the book is 135,000; consequently, Vonnegut claims that more people died that night than at any other moment in history. But he takes the figures from David Irving's book *The Destruction of Dresden*, which deliberately inflated the figures so as to comply with Irving's sympathetic portrayal of the Nazis. The actual figure, established by enquiries set in motion by the Dresden city authorities many years later, is probably nearer 25,000 to 30,000. The Nazis themselves insisted it had been 200,000, but that had been for their own immediate propaganda purposes. If anyone should have known, surely it should have been Vonnegut himself? After all he was there; he didn't need to consult anyone else's text. But how could he have known? Was he meant to go and count all the piles of black ash? Or ask around amongst the dazed survivors, hunting for their relatives?

And so Vonnegut never changed the figures in the book, even though he must have come to know subsequently about the discrediting of Irving's statistics. He presumably felt that the truth of that text of his did not depend, one way or the other, upon the accuracy of the figures of fatality. The truth of the book lies in its portrayal of the insane destructiveness of war. That truth survives any other inaccuracies. Now a curious thing has happened with the Gospel of John. Matthew Arnold could greatly admire its rhetorical power, but he thought the topography depicted in it was nothing less than a fantasy. The text here, he reckoned, was unsound. Modern archaeology has proved him wrong there. Excavations have shown that the pool of Bethesda was precisely where John said it was. Ditto the pavement from which Pontius Pilate delivered his judgment. Does this make the Gospel more or less true? After all, we do not go to John to map Jerusalem. We go to find the identity of Jesus. (Actually we go to find the identity of Christ, since John's text is at least as preoccupied with the transhistorical redeemer as it is with the historical preacher and healer.)

The only truth any text can generate is one that arises out of its form, function, and historical placement.

The only truth any text can generate is one that arises out of its form, function, and historical placement. If we could take Einstein's famous equation back to ancient Rome, its meaning would be entirely unfathomable. Its terms can only be read through the findings of modern science. And here we should distinguish detail from truth. If we could establish that John's dating of the trial and execution of Jesus was more correct in detail day by day than that of the synoptics, then that would indeed confirm the details of his text, but not the 'truth' of it. In the same way that the truth embodied in Vonnegut's novel survives his miscalculation of the Dresden deaths.

TEXTUALITY: EPHESUS AND PATMOS

If scripture is questioned and worried at by midrash, what happens when literature comes along? The term 'literature' here means simply written down, as opposed to being transmitted by an oral tradition. But it has come to mean something different. It has come to mean a text freer even than midrash to interpret what is presented to it in terms of tradition and experience. Literature can be midrashic; midrash can never entirely risk the freedom of literature, and we can normally see the difference between the classifications. The portrayal of Jesus by Blake, in all its antinomian vigour, would prompt most Christians to say that he has left the realm of midrash, and entered the freer world of literature. Blake has severed those anchoring connections with scripture and tradition which indicate subscription to a credal system. The first person of the trinity, for Blake, is simply Old Nobodaddy; a projection of our negativities and fears into a cosmic personage of law and punishment.

In chapters 21 to 24 of Deuteronomy we are given Moses in all his scriptural glory. He points out to the Israelites that the law he has given them must be written on their hearts, or they will once more go whoring after strange gods. He sings the song he himself has composed. Then he gazes over the Jordan from Mount Nebo at the land of promise Yahweh has told him he'll never set foot in. Then he dies. It is one of the most sublime moments in the Bible. Moses is, according to tradition, closing the Pentateuch. The great narrative will now be continued by Joshua.

MIDRASH HAS AN inexhaustible source here. But beyond midrash we encounter far more dangerous ground. Having escaped the Nazis in Vienna, Sigmund Freud arrived in England and promptly set to work demolishing the foundations of the religion which had attempted to nurture him. He wrote a book, *Moses and Monotheism*, which argued strongly that Moses was not a Jew at all, but a patrician Egyptian. The evidence cited for this, which is characteristic of Freud's later metapsychology, is linguistic, anthropological, and mythographic. Freud was only uttering what had come to be a well-rehearsed anthropological argument of his day. All the same, his endeavours caused alarm. At this, the most perilous moment for the Jewish people in modern times, the most famous living Jew on earth was about to suggest that the Jewish faith was founded on a misconception. Even worse, Freud went on to argue that so harsh was the law Moses imposed on the Israelites in the desert, and so bitterly unwelcome, that they killed him. And he reckoned they had dealt with their suppressed guilt by their paradoxical piety towards his person ever afterwards. Thus does our duplicitous psyche make amends. Abraham Yahuda pleaded with him not to publish; Freud was having none of it. *Quod scripsi, scripsi*. The Roman Catholic Church was not best pleased either. The Dominican Vincent McNabb wondered in print if this was the most gracious way for a Jewish refugee to thank Great Britain for taking him in at such a time of peril.

By the time we get to a text like *Moses and Monotheism*, we are no longer dealing with midrash. Midrash has been overtaken by a species of analysis which has snapped the thread which holds a tradition together. So has this now left behind scripture and midrash, and become instead literature? Well, it soon would be, even in terms of genre classifications. During the war Thomas Mann was invited to contribute a story to an American volume entitled *The Ten Commandments*. Over six weeks he wrote a novella, *The Tablets of the Law*. The rest of the book has been long-forgotten, but Mann's piece is still an exemplary example of fiction that engages scripture with utter seriousness, but without feeling the constraints of any traditional pieties.

Mann knew his Freud well. He had delivered the address when Freud was awarded the Goethe Prize, and wrote an essay entitled 'Freud's Position', which is a brilliant approach to Freud's achievement. And *The Tablets of the Law* has Freud immediately behind it, in the form of *Moses and Monotheism*. This Moses is the illegitimate son of a Hebrew labourer and the daughter of the Pharaoh; her wayward aristocratic passion costs the poor fellow his life. Out of the warring identities inside Moses comes the figure we know, devoted to his curious god of invisibility. But this is no longer midrash; it has become literature. Just as midrash passes over into literature in Robert Browning's 'A Death in the Desert', where the aged John is close to death, tended lovingly by his disciples, contemplating what it means that the last living contact with Jesus is finally about to die.

The interactions between revelation and philosophy, between interpretation and analysis, between scripture and literature, are ceaseless, and not always measurable. Only in John's gospel are we treated to the exposition of Jesus as logos. Why might this be? The tradition has held that John spent time (perhaps even the rest of his life) in Ephesus. And Ephesus was in some ways the home of the logos. Heraclitus had been there five centuries before, pondering how the scheme of creation is only intelligible at all because of its structuring through the logos; how logos is a mediation between the absolute of the godhead and the temporal and physical rootedness of human intellection. And then Philo of Alexandria had been in Ephesus at the time of John and Jesus, saying something remarkably similar. So it is at the least possible that the reason we have Jesus described as the logos is because he was being written about in

Ephesus after his death; there is no evidence that he ever spoke thus of himself. That was not at all a part of the text he was expounding while he lived.

So here, it would seem, scripture itself is being shaped by the literature of philosophy. What Jesus effectively says in the story of the woman taken in adultery is this: the law is never separate from the agency enacting it, and that is you. Do not act as though the law can be separated from your imaginations, or your interpretations or your desires. For that is a form of idolatry. In this sublime moment, scripture, midrash and literature all become one. The text we are writing is the text of our own lives.

2. THE PATMOS DICTATIONS

My mind's turned dark and allegorical.

Words mangled into strange constructions
fashioned by my secretary here. He hears my secrets
each late afternoon, then writes them down
laboriously in our cellar overnight
to the solitary scratching of a rat's chorus.

Ungrammatical his script may be
but this crabbed apocalypse could cost us both our lives
(mine I would happily relinquish).
That gospel I dictated too
(no need for fishermen to write –
what is there to be writ on water?)
but there one learned rabbi billeted in Ephesus

honeycombed my koiné with his scriptural allusions
leaving enough of my Aramaic meditations
to show beneath the surface like a rising Galilean shoal.

The Lord spoke Aramaic in the intimacy of his parables.
Only in cities, near the Temple, or propounding
from some Galilean hill
did his mouth mint coins for them
uttering the tribute money of the Caesars.
The language of our lords and masters.
Oppression's tongue can still yield metaphors
as Kafka transmutes the cockroach
into a sentient and tragic protagonist.
Two decades later Heydrich moved to Prague.
Cockroaches, awaiting starvation in the ghetto.
The word its own prolepsis, then as now.

Such a devoted disciple, you write down
whatever fresh images torment me, though
rendered in the crudest letters. I'm no penman
but can hear each sound the words make
when you read them back. They're crooked.
You stumbled, my lad, while you learned your abecedary.
No remedy for this now. Here's what we'll bequeath.
Once I listened as he made each word
explode like old suns, done at last with shining
throwing themselves at darkness in a final flourish.

Candelabra seven-branched sent back as booty
to imperial Rome. Accoutrement for the next triumphal

arch.
Men women children self-slaughtered at Masada.
And he who promised to be back before
we'd counted to a hundred
still not here. Now heavens fill with emblems.
Rome even dictates a change in the weather.
Ravens fall out of a blackened sky
on creaking wings. Ocean waves
describe a dragon's tail
lashing away its salt detritus.
Dragons whores and Babylon
while I'm mewed up in my melancholy
a dizzard fondling his Bedlam chains
waiting for the shilling to be spent.

You listen to my breathing
in the night sometimes, when you are done
scratching away at the parchment
trying so hard not to blot it.
I hear you barefooting across the boards
to eavesdrop on my ancient heart; to auscultate
and sigh: The old man's not gone yet;
we'll get another day's dictation
as shadows hunger round his tomb.

How many days
how many decades
did they gather round
in Mary's tiny house at Ephesus
while she sat by the window

waiting for the sun to drop out of the sky?
Day by day
he walked out of the darkness of his death
as a man walks smiling - his shroud intact -
into a gospel future.
City of Artemis.
One breast for every free hand in the market.
When Paul arrived here, thrashing about the areopagus,
they twitched, those silversmiths who make her votive offerings,
fingering their leather wallets.
He'd never met the Lord, you know,
and never did grasp what I meant by LOGOS.
He should have stayed in Ephesus as long as I did:
Herakleitos. Philo. Hard to escape: dust in the alley.
Each of his words a bird on the wing
carried by thermals over the abyss
and not a single feather fell
but his father in heaven would catch it and blow.
The wind's bravado is its own apocalypse.
Meteorology translated to catastrophe.
Hear Marduk smashing the skull of Tiamat
with every sizzling breaker.

Could the earth have died with him?
Mineral veins fossilized
green sap once
forced through. Like Artemis
he turns into his own stiff effigy
to which the pilgrims make obeisance

while Empire's pterodactyls hover overhead
drones ready to drop exploding metal eggs
on Pashtun villages.
Patmos is here and everywhere.
All times and now.
The island you can never flee; its sea a noose
tightened round the future's neck.

So many years ago
it is another lifetime
I stood on a hill above the Dead Sea.
Out of a querulous mist the Qumran brothers
strode, vigorous in self-denial
loathing every moving shape beyond their hallowed walls:
sons of darkness; beslimers of the Law
caged in this world's bestiary.
A different species.
And I stood riddled in forgiveness
alone as the mist embraced me.
Caspar David Friedrich could have painted this
as Schumann's fractured melodies rebuked the scathing
wind.
Now we pour wine
to close this private seminar.
Listen to the storm's effrontery outside
shaking trees as though they were
recalcitrant witnesses
standing dumb before the vernal Emperor.
The skies tonight are chaos.
Let the world's dark emblems

talk themselves into exhaustion.
Maranatha.
He poured once at the table
for his beloved disciple
and I would drink it down.
A shared transfusion.

Note the cup's kenosis:
emptying itself
then filling up again.
Each day now
I count another resurrection.

3. THE CULT AT EPHESUS

MORE THAN TWENTY years after his death, I first went to see the dream-shaper. Told him I wanted the labyrinth of my mind prepared for the Lord's re-entry. He could clear away whatever lumber and rubble he chose, just as long as I'd encounter once more the healer from Galilee in the streets of darkness that are my dreams.

We have been in Ephesus for all of these years. I had taken his mother, as he had instructed, and we had cleared out of Judaea. We travelled north, but Galilee was altogether too riddled with memories for both of us. So we came here. Where the synagogue was happy enough to hear from us at first. But now they show us the door. They could allow that he might be a messiah. But not the Messiah. There've been so many, you see, coming and going, closing the door on time. Now they say we are a cult, to be deprecated. At the mere sight of us they utter anathemas. Dark reports are delivered to officials in Jerusalem.

My followers call our home the House of the Interpreter. They come once a week in the evening, and I read to them from the scroll he left. He spoke in Aramaic and Koinē, sometimes in alternate lines, as when he gave the mountainside blessings. (Our spirits were bilingual in those days.) But only ever wrote in Aramaic, and when there was nobody else around, except the Beloved Disciple. That's me. And then he gave me the scroll, the night before they came to take him. It took years for me to learn to read my way through without stumbling, and to this day I can't write. The two sons of Zebedee had no need to read and write. The old man taught us to count up to a hundred, so we knew how many fish were in each net, but reading and writing: that was for scribes. The ones with no dirt beneath their fingernails. They scratch things down for me on parchment, my followers; that's for the codex. But only I am permitted to hold the scroll and read out his words. And when I die, it is to be buried with me: that was his requirement and request. They call me the Eagle. Only the Eagle, you see, can look into the sun and not be blinded.

She sits over by the window, and stares into the cup of wine I poured her. Seldom drinks. Only stares. As if the wine were about to speak. In one language or the other.

TODAY IT HAPPENED, finally. The dream-shaper is a man named Alexis. Of no known faith, with a beard as variegated as the rocks around Qumran. When he stares into your eyes you become luminous and vacant, as though thieves had come and emptied the house in your head of all its furniture. And then set fire to it. His extasis; your kenosis. The hours stop moving. The dark side of the moon begins to whisper to you in an unknown language. Beckoning.

'First we will empty you. Only then will what you want arrive. To be filled you must be emptied first.' That was what he always said, too. I sometimes wonder if the shaper simply finds words inside me then gives them back, as echoes. Today Alexis says: 'I think you need to meet the Logos Man. The Alexandrian philosopher. A fellow called Philo.'

'How would I do that?'

'He has just arrived from Egypt. He will be here in a moment.' And in a moment he is.

A feud today between high winds and waves. So when the Alexandrian speaks, his lips are already salted with acerbity as well as love. This is Philo from over the seas.

He sits and stares at me. I sit and stare at him. His bald head a shiny dome, a basilica's roof after rain. Eyes: two amethysts that have swallowed a flaming torch apiece. And a beard that harbours no philosophical doubt, a beard that certainly knows its own mind regarding anything and everything. Each thought uttered out of that beard stiffens its bristles in assertion. Juts its chin. In the beginning was Logos. And at the end as well. The teaching of Herakleitos five centuries ago, and in this very town. His smile bright as a sun in summer.

Philo beckons me outside, into the garden. Alexis nods for me to go, though he stays behind.

'Look, my friend. The tree is earth's answer to heaven's light and water. That's how Logos translates heaven into earth.

'Now if he met you there by the Lake of Galilee, then that was Logos alive among the living. Talking with his mouth. Fishing with hungry fishermen. But now he has passed through death. Now he must come to you in dreams and visions. So you must prepare a Logos-shaped basilica inside your sleeping mind to receive him. Alexis has been helping you, he tells me. He is already there, your Lord, I can see that, but he remains exiled, flickering in pale flames: consumed in the Gehenna of your affections. You are still bitter at his fate, and he never counselled that. You cannot see him in such a *tohu-wabohu* desert of incomprehension. Logos awaits his invitation: he never forces an entry. But with eagle eyes and the ant's diligence, you will arrive. Arrive at the place where you first started. And count the fish once more.' He pauses for a moment now. 'Did he really do all the things they say, my friend?'

'I watched as the powers left the tormented one in Gadara. As though a darkness bigger than the night flew out of his mouth, his nose and his ears. A flock of bats so vast that it cancelled day and sunlight, and then they were gone into the pigs, the herd that froze for a second as though they would all fall over, and then ran for the water. The comfort of drowning. Anything but to have that darkness scorching you like hot coals burning right through your belly.'

'I bet the pig-man was not best pleased.'

'No. He did not become a disciple that day. Went and told the Roman landlord that he'd never pay him now. Another casualty of the Decapolis. The pigs were for the legionnaires. No worries about kosher food with those boys.' I can feel his spirit now as he locks on to something inside my skull.

'How did you lose your smile?'

TEXTUALITY: EPHESUS AND PATMOS

I was not expecting this. I try to explain. How a moment comes in every life when irony must die. When the double-dealing miscreant on the stage stops grinning. When the dark side of each word's moon stops offering its lunar escape. That day on Golgotha. When we looked up to see the angels descending in glory to raise him up. And they never arrived. As we put him in the linen shroud, Joseph of Arimathea said: 'The grave will never be able to hold him.'

We'd needed a drink, all of us, believe me, when we finally reassembled, after all the hours of torture and execution that day. But when it came at last there were dead flies floating on the wine's bloody surface. One sip turned to wormwood and gall. We all threw the contents of our cups on the ground. And only then did we see the earth's red wounds. His death now part of the landscape.

'I think he might want you to start smiling again. It will begin any moment. In your dreams tonight. You are ready to encounter Logos.'

Am I? Already in Jerusalem, I hear, tabernacle toadies have started to misquote me. And I have never used this word. This word they all keep uttering.

AROUND THE TEMENOS of Artemis's temple you can buy statues of every kind. Gold silver bronze. Painted clay for the poor man. But particularly silver. Women bury them inside their clothes or down in the black holes between the bedsheets, so as to ensure fertility, as the deed is done in darkness. This week he came here, preaching before the temple. Until they ran him out of town, the silver merchants, sensing a serious threat to their livelihoods, nervously fingering their leather money pouches. He never came near us, and we never went near him. He who never met the Lord in life, but will now teach the whole wide world about him; those who spoke no Aramaic at all. The word among us is that it was Paul, or Saul as he was then called, who cast the first stone at Stephen, the first of us to die for the faith. Saul, filled as he was then with the Law's malignancy. And now he says all that has gone, gone with the dawn tide, to be replaced by love. Which throws him from his horse and blinds him.

Artemis. She has a breast for every shyster from here to the moon, selling his sacred trinkets. Some of the daintier ones round here insist they are not breasts at all, but the ova of the sacred bee. Well, they look like breasts to me. On her feast days, this place is Babel. Give the preacher credit where it's due: he's not short on courage to have gone down there to preach, with so many of her devotees hovering around, frisky as hornets. And now he's gone again, leaving us to pick up the pieces. He who threw the first stone. In Jerusalem they laughed whenever we opened our mouths.

'Ignorant pigs. What can they know of the law or the spirit? They can't even speak so that anyone but a pig can understand them. Send them all back to Galilee where they belong.'

The ventriloquists of human contentment have been at their anaesthetic toils. All will be well, etc. Not here, it won't. Anyone telling you so is a snake-oil merchant. A gargoyle disfiguring the cathedral's sacrifice. Even though there are as yet no cathedrals. But there will be, believe me. My dreams have begun now, as the shaper predicted, and they inform me of days to come.

She has already gone to bed. I sit in the chair and do what the shaper has taught me. Concentrate so hard on a memory that I enter it, and it enters me. We are back in Samaria. The two of us. He needs a rest from crowds who sluice the sacred out of him, as though he were a wadi, rushing suddenly across a dust-dry plain. He stares up at the sky.

'I saw Satan falling from heaven.'

'How did he look?'

'Like a great bird hit by lead slingshot.'

And at some point I fall asleep, and he is walking through the streets of darkness in my mind. The darkness immediately falls away.

They have brought her before him for condemnation on the Sabbath. So he can only write in dust. Anyone writing two letters together on that day would be liable to condemnation, according to the ancient law of the Rabbis. But writing in the dust, where the words cannot remain for longer than an hour – that is deemed permissible. He could also have written in water, fruit juice or soft cheese. But it is in dust that he writes. *Quia pulvis est.* Writes their names, these accusers, and their chief sins, which far exceed any darkness inside the weeping adulteress. They read their condemnation in the dust, one by one, and they leave, as he kicks over the traces of the script at his feet. The words of their expulsion vanish now, just as the words of her condemnation have vanished too. Into the dust; into the air. Thus law is overwhelmed at last by forgiveness. Thus did the light shine, and the dark comprehended it not, but it never overcame it either. For this is Logos, and now I understand, as if for the first time.

The day arrives with Roman trumpets, lictors and street glories. It is beribboned. Even the sky is dressed up like a dog's dinner. Celebrating Caesar in his pomp and glory. A breakfast for ravens; ashes for the quick. What's left over will sink and be vermiculated. Now that true dreams have started I know that I live at last in the realm of the Prolific and the Devourer. One speaks life only, and the other swallows it. In the corner a cockroach is eating a speckle of bread. That last white crumb of meaning consumed by the shiny black body. Alpha. Omega. White page black ink. By the time we arrive at the bottom of the page, he might have returned.

When my little flock turn up this day, I have something new to tell them. I recount to them the new story, the one he returned to in my dream, so as to remind me. To recapitulate. My dracophobic followers do not wish to spend eternity in the inferno that is the flaming gut of the dragon. They are avid for any news of mercy and atonement.

'Why have you never told us this before?'

'Perhaps the time was not right before. But now it is. Let he who is without sin cast the first stone.'

Stylus scratches over parchment. Then I stare hard at the scroll, even though I am not reading from it. The words have been written inside me and are translating themselves now on to my tongue. I have been imprinted. I do not want to confuse them, these fierce and loyal friends of mine.

'And there's something else. Something that needs to be inserted. Please write it down.

'In the beginning was Logos, and Logos was with God; and Logos was God. At the very beginning there with Him. All things, you see, were made by Logos and through Logos, and without Logos nothing that was made was made. Life was in it, shining, and this life was the light of all men. And the light shines in the dark, but the dark can never baffle it. We were made through Logos. So we are one with Logos. Sons of light not of darkness.'

'Shall we put this at the end, Teacher?'

'No. At the beginning, I think.'

THEY ALL LEAVE finally. I sit and stare through the window all night. In this dwelling-pace of intermediate spirits, hovering. Awaiting the dictation of Logos. Seeing light in the darkness out there. I stare into the polished metal and see an old man staring back at me. Grey beard. Eagle eyes. That old man is me, but not yet. Not yet.

So much is now written inside me. The plaited lines of a luminous manuscript seem to knot and then unknot their braids, as each tide swallows another mouthful of an island away in the north somewhere. Dreams are carrying me forward into time. I can read (with such ease, suddenly) their insular minuscule. Keep it so small that only a migrant preacher would even notice such words, as they scurry from holes in the rock, where the dragon's breath can't scorch them any more.

Dawn is pulling back the sheets. The cup of wine I poured her sits still on the wooden table. She never touched a drop. I drink it off and sit down to read what they wrote last night. Still a little space on the parchment they left behind. We've not reached the bottom of the page. Yet.

CHAPTER NOTE

If it is an interpolation, then the interpolator was one of genius. The story encapsulates the way Jesus constantly turns the Law around, so that those who would prosecute it, find themselves disqualified from condemnation by their own evident imperfections.

14.

Tolerance and Form

ALL REPRESENTATION IS permitted by the tolerance and generosity of the quantum. Energy arrives in specific forms, dictated by the quantum states. It cannot subsist between one state and another. There is no half-way state: if there is, it is a wasteland. The most primal form of the cosmos is, precisely, formalist in its demands and its permissions. Be thus or be thus, it says, but you can't be unthus. And when energy ceases to exist in its specific forms, so do we.

And yet, the history of representation is the history of tolerance. No representation, artistic or scientific, is exact. The only 'exact' representation of a man would be three-dimensional and the same size as a man. A sculpture then? No, because we all know how different a sculpture is from a man. Stone is not like flesh, neither is metal or even plastic. And a sculpture does not move like a man. Nor does its face display alert intelligence; nor does its mouth speak truths to power. All forms of representation are formal distortions and simplifications: each form is different from every other. All formal modes operate according to their own laws. And we must agree to exist perceptually within those forms for the duration. Otherwise the energy dissipates, disperses into the chaos of formlessness.

Borges enjoyed himself with this theme in 'On Exactitude in Science', a very short story. It provides the chronicle of a land where the mapmakers became so obsessive, so demented in their pursuit of exactitude, that they would only finally be satisfied with a map which coincided inch for inch with the land it was representing. So that was a true, an exact, representation. It was therefore utterly useless. It had forgotten why we make representations in the first place: for intellectual convenience or glorification. We make images that fit in some way into the sensorium. Nell Gwynne might have gone for a while, but Charles II still has a portrait of her in oils on his bedchamber wall. Not that he can take it to bed, exactly, but it is a usefully sensuous mnemonic, all the same. Reminds him who he might summon the next morning, should he need to exercise his *droit de seigneur*.

Jacob Bronowski argued that the Principle of Uncertainty would have been better named the Principle of Tolerance. The relationship between the position of a particle and its acceleration is contained by the tolerance permitted within the terms of the quantum. If I see this aspect exactly, then that aspect becomes inexact. A photographer at the time would have understood this well enough. I can see everything in focus, but only from a wide enough angle in the lens. If I want close-up tight focus, then everything around will become relatively unfocused. These are the terms of perception, and also of representation. Here we have the tolerance of a lens. We always see through lenses; our eyes are lenses...

What is the end of representation? To say that this is in fact that. To bring everything within our intellectual manipulations. To say, as Bob Dylan had it, that every distance, however far, is near. The orrery brings the planets within the span of our arms. Human thought, we assert, brings everything, however vast, distant and mighty, within the sensorium. We miniaturise the cosmos by representing it. With the letters of our language and the numbers from zero to nine, we can calculate and convey the whole. In printing terms that's only thirty-six glyphs. You can fit them on to two lines. A pretty minimal resource with which to convey everything that ever was – not to mention everything that ever will be.

Linguistic form is the most flexible type of representation. Walter Benjamin called it non-sensuous mimesis. The cosmos is translated into an encyclopaedia. We like to assume that our representations are self-identical with the object represented; they never are. Each form asserts its own particular terms for identity. Every quiddity, formally translated, becomes a quiddity removed by one step. A cinematic experience of a war is not at all the same as the experience of actually being in the war. We are not about to be blasted out of our seats. Bullets do not stream from the screen. We do not hear our children scream, unless it's for popcorn or ice cream. And yet we grant the representation a certain validity: precisely, the validity of representation. This is a validity based on tolerance. So does such representation have any limits set upon it?

Claude Lanzmann believed that we had reached the end of representation when it came to the Holocaust. He said, pretty definitively: representation stops here; all you can do is faithfully record the traces. Here representation can only ever falsify. A healthy actor playing a starving concentration camp victim is not a truth. Here we confront the terminus of representation. Here we see what it can't do as well as what it can.

In the apophatic theological tradition, you can't meaningfully say anything about what God is; you can only say what He isn't. To say what He is, is to overestimate the size and capacity of our language. It is to assume it can contain what in fact contains it. Lanzmann was perhaps apophatic about the camps. A positive representation of them was a lie. All you could do was trace the remains; attend to the testimonies, or even prompt the testimonies, as with the barber in Tel Aviv, who pleads not to have to go on, but Lanzmann won't let him finish. His dreadful testimony must be told. Otherwise, history vanishes before our eyes, never to return. History exists here only in relief — in its negative traces. Pursued by an unrelenting inquisitor.

But towards the end Lanzmann made an exception to his own rule. This was the film *Son of Saul*. He never explained fully why he was prepared to bestow upon this representation of the Shoah his imprimatur. In this film Lāszl Nemes follows his character, Saul Ausländer, relentlessly as he battles through life in the camps, day by day, hour by hour. The actor barely acts, or so it seems; he simply pursues his role, his fate, grimly, minute by minute. And he is usually the only one who is fully in focus; the other figures around him are soft. When a camera closes in to a close-up on a face, everything around that face half-vanishes. This is the optical exclusion principle. The face enlarges into its own world. It entirely fills the space of our tolerance. Bronowski, as we noted, said the Uncertainty Principle should become the Principle of Toleration. The more I focus on this, the more that goes out of focus. We can see Saul but only at the expense of other people going out of focus, bodies both living and dead. The film thus embodies a perceptual truth. We can only keep one man entirely in focus. And he can only keep himself entirely in focus.

Nature, however we construe it, is inescapable. I draw a tree upon a sheet of paper. I am drawing a tree on a tree, just as I once etched the outline of a narwhal upon a narwhal's tusk. When I sit at my computer and describe electrons and plastic, electrons and plastic have played their part in my computerised description. There is no pure intellect. Flesh and blood mediate each thought. Breathing plays its part in every mental transaction. There is no representation that can be separated from the mediation of humanity.

Shakespeare is a thinker, who thought through plays and poetry. He was not a philosopher. He did not write works of philosophy, nor (as far as we can see) did he wish to. Imagine what King Lear would be, 'translated into philosophy'. We already knew it all, philosophically speaking; but we knew nothing except abstractions. It is the representation of figures (most of whom never 'existed' in the first place) that makes us journey through this arid and terrifying region of thought. This is a dramatist thinking, and drama is the form of his thought. If there are certainties in *Lear*, they are shaken out of their wits by the end. If this were a philosophy, it would self-explode. Tolerance is here at war with certainty.

Shakespeare's language is more vivid and truthful than a philosopher's, because it leaks. It erodes its boundaries. Simile runs to metaphor. One voice turns into another. The language is crowded with presences; it never seeks to purge itself of contingency, as philosophy does. Instead, it accepts contingency as the realm in which we live. It understands the provisionality of everything we say, however absolute we might imagine that saying to be. Metaphors leap out of sentences like caged beasts when the trap is sprung. Cassius describes how Caesar was sick. The blood ran out of his lips, but this becomes: 'His coward lips did from their colour fly.' Every bodily part becomes a member of an army in terrified retreat. Such metaphorical profusion represents what? Merely, how fecund the imagery of the mind becomes when heated up to match the subject. The representation has spurted into unpredictable variegation. Representation asserts its own independent being. It becomes self-generating. It is no longer tied to a specific 'signified'. Rather it spawns its own signifieds. Here now is a manifold facility for independent signification.

All the same, thisness has been translated into that thatness, and it can only do this by changing form. Whenever something changes form it is no longer what it was when it started. I take human beings and convert them into celluloid; I take a woman and convert her into paint and canvas; I take a life and turn it into a volume of printed words. Change a form, change an identity. This is true in physics; it is also true in art. And yet the identities can share a form. This is what we mean when we say: this is a truthful representation of Caesar. An existential form is still maintained between them.

We remember the Borges story 'On exactitude in Science'. If in our representation there is no tolerance and no play, then that representation becomes useless. It is not a representation at all; it is a mere replication. Replication represents sterility. The history of representation is based on tolerance. Take the tolerance away, and I say, 'Look here is a picture of Guernica.' Reply: 'No it isn't. It's a picture of a bull, a young woman with a candle, a picador's horse, disembowelled. There's a lightbulb – that's as realistic as the whole thing ever becomes.' Only tolerance allows the transcendence of this reductive dismissal. Only tolerance permits an allegory to somehow 'represent' an event involving aircraft in 1936. For after all, what does *Guernica* represent? Hardly modernity. The most modern thing in it is the lightbulb. You could also perhaps include the dashes (added by Dora Maar) that might represent newsprint, but newsprint had been around for three hundred years. Most of the other things in it could have come out of *Minotauramachy*, of 1935. That utterly brilliant etching came into being before Guernica ever happened. Yet this is the art of modernity. Yet so was the bombing. Von Richthofen, who led the attack, exulted in the 'splendid modernity' of the foray.

To go back to where we started, the more exactly we can see the position of the electron, the less can we identify its speed. The more accurately we can track its speed, the less precisely we can focus its position. This is the uncertainty factor; or as Bronowski would have put it, we require tolerance to cope with this or any other bifocal perception. And all our perceptions are to some degree bifocal. So the Principle of Tolerance could also be called the Principle of Focus. The more I focus on one thing, the less the others are sharp. The more I look hard at this, the less I see that. The modernist shock to the Victorian sensibility showed how intolerant certain human eyes had become. They had been overtrained in a certain type of focusing, or tradition. Modernism therefore presented them with forms that were unintelligible to them, even though these forms were much more 'foundational' for human perception.

Any practised cameraman knows that if you focus hard on one thing, other things go relatively out of focus. In *Son of Saul*, Ausländer stays visually hard while all the figures around him soften. Tolerance permits uncertainty. Certainty is inherently intolerant. Heisenberg's Principle of Uncertainty is, as Bronowski insisted, a way of describing the tolerance of the quantum.

Uncertainty requires provisionality. Certainty is Borges's useless map covering every inch of the 'represented country'. Such a perfect representation is of no use whatsoever. Like certainty. All our perceptions are ultimately permitted by the quantum, and that requires a certain tolerance. We should always beware our own sentences and our own images. Those representations from the Hubble Telescopes were carefully put together from a variety of sources: no human being has ever 'seen' these images until they were actually constructed as images. All representation is dependent on the modalities of knowledge. How we perceive and know is shaped inexorably by the form of whatever it is that is being represented, but also by the means of representation. The sharing of forms in different modalities facilitates knowledge. And it requires tolerance.

Energy is formalist. It will not dissipate itself in any quantity or in any direction. It arrives in specified forms, in specific frequencies and quotients. We call these forms the quantum states. Classical physics had assumed there could be no breaks in nature; that all its atomic movements should therefore be seamless. No gaps, no jumps. But the quantum introduced jumps, and therefore discontinuities. Within the terms of the quantum, certain tolerances are permitted; others are not. So if I seek to know the precise position of a particle, then I cannot simultaneously know its velocity, and consequently I can see Saul Ausländer in his granular hardness, or I can see the others thus. But I can't see both.

Because energy is intolerant of formlessness, it congregates in distinctive shapes. Tolerance is a species of formalism. We assess how much 'play' there is in any situation, and exploit it. Knowledge of the form, and a brave exploration of its dimensions, allows for the maximum of artistic motion. Without this, we end up with Borges's dread kingdom. Where there is no representation only replication. No creation; only cloning. You will get what it says on the tin; what it always said on the tin. Genesis is now a template; unalterable. Nothing here can thrive or improvise. In the Borges map there is no play, only unrelenting replication. This is a sterile world of repeated perfections. This is where Nature becomes its own pastiche.

In any sexual relationship, there is a perennial tension between desire and respect. Should these two go seriously out of kilter, they become mere co-morbidities. In words, tolerance is the journey travelled between the etymological get-go and current usage. We could list examples. When Chaucer used the word *silly* (*sely*) it meant free of sin. Uncontaminated. The meaning has now changed along with the spelling. Internecine originally meant damaging to both sides not mutually destructive. And how about nice? Coming to us from the Latin *nescire*, meaning to not know, it meant at one time stupid or ignorant. Then for a time it meant precise or fastidious. We have retained this usage (only just) in our phrase, That's a nice point. Now the word simply means the opposite of unpleasant. It has become a directive item of the lexicon

Tolerance is a generous exploration of form. If you accept things with no interest in their form, that is not tolerance, it is breeziness. Accepting people with no real interest in the form of their spirits is not tolerance either; it is simply a blurry inclusiveness. Jesus suggests tolerance through dialectical perception. He says: try to see what's seen, but also what's doing the seeing and why. Don't spot the mote in your brother's eye while being blind to the beam in your own. Do unto others as you would be done unto. Forgive the trespasses of others as you would have your own trespasses forgiven. The observer changes the object observed, and that's where the tolerance comes in. Jesus had seen that long before quantum mechanics.

If he had been around in Galileo's time, Jesus might well have said: Make sure you are looking at your companions through the right end of the telescope. Or they might look at you through the wrong end of their constellation of lenses too. Then we'll all be Lilliputians crawling over the corpus of a giant, even if we do call that massive body tradition.

Alan Wall *was born in Bradford, studied English at Oxford, lives in North Wales and is currently Professor of Writing and Literature at the University of Chester. He has published six novels and three collections of poetry, including Doctor Placebo. Jacob, a book written in verse and prose, was shortlisted for the Hawthornden Prize. His work has been translated into ten languages. He has published essays and reviews in many different periodicals including the* Guardian, Spectator, The Times, Jewish Quarterly, Leonardo, PN Review, London Magazine, The Reader *and* Agenda. *He was Royal Literary Fund Fellow in Writing at Warwick University and Liverpool John Moores and is a contributing editor of* The Fortnightly Review. *His book Endtimes was published by Shearsman in 2013, and Badmouth, a novel, was published by Harbour Books in 2014. This is the third collection of his essays published by Odd Volumes,* The Fortnightly Review's *publishing imprint.*

Alan Wall's trilogy of *Fortnightly* essays

Labyrinths & Clues (May 2014)

Walter Benjamin: An Arcade of Reflections (June 2018)

Midnight of the Sublime: Essays& Reviews (March 2021)

Available from all booksellers or the publisher:

Odd Volumes
The Fortnightly Review

Le Ligny
85260 Les Brouzils
France

www.fortnightlyreview.co.uk

www.ingramcontent.com/pod-product-compliance
Lightning Source LLC
Chambersburg PA
CBHW071112160426
43196CB00013B/2546